"Financial indepen [barcode] accomplished this through the Singapore stock, deep research, due diligence and being on top of your investments, pay dividends. Not one to sit on the sidelines, he is well-known as a crusader for investors, grilling listed company boards and management with facts, figures and good questions at annual general meetings. By actively participating, he is often a welcome voice of reason."

— Chew Sutat
Executive Vice President (Equities & Fixed Income),
Singapore Exchange

"Financial literacy is an essential skill, yet most people do not have it. It is not that we should all aspire to be like Warren Buffett, but with longer life spans, an ageing society and increasing healthcare costs, everyone needs to understand how to manage their financial resources. Mano's background makes him eminently qualified to comment on this important topic, to draw the distinction between investing and speculating, and it is my hope that his audience will not be limited to only those who are already financially literate."

— Koh Boon Hwee
Distinguished corporate leader, entrepreneur
and investor, and former Chairman of SingTel
and Singapore Airlines

"Multi-skilled financial expert Mano Sabnani (journalist, financial analyst, company director, activist investor) has produced a no-nonsense book on financial planning and investment, which should be mandatory reading for every budding analyst or investor. Interestingly, rather than guaranteeing vast riches for every reader – which are the usual claims of other authors – Sabnani is modest enough to promise only financial freedom and no longer being 'slaves in a globalised world'. It is a book that will empower you whatever your income or educational level."

— Ho Kwon Ping
Executive Chairman of Banyan Tree Holdings and
Chairman of Singapore Management University

What Other Successful Investors Say...

"Sincere, open, and insightful, Mano has been investing for decades, has reached financial freedom and comfortably supported a happy family. You will see all these attributes in the wisdom he shares in this easy-to-read book. For those who have not started investing, his case study of how a middle-income family making $8.8 k per month can build up total assets of $1.8 m should motivate you to start. After all, knowing that we don't have to rely on job income gives us true freedom to pursue our dreams."

— Tan Wey Ling
Former VP Asia for Syniverse

"Most Singapore investors will know Mano as a champion of minority shareholders and fearless in raising pertinent business issues at company AGMs. His latest book is filled with practical advice for successful investing, from navigating investment pitfalls and cultivating emotional discipline to proper asset allocation. I am a fan of Mano's investing acumen."

— Goh Han Peng
Director, R3 Asset Management

"Investing in yourself is the best investment you will ever make, and it is always helpful to have someone like Mano who can guide you. His views on financial matters are practical in application and expressed in plain and simple language. I would highly recommend *Mano Sabnani's Money Secrets* to anyone who is looking for a simple and easy read to improve their financial literacy and to benefit from Mano's vast experience."

— Deepak Ramchandani
SVP, Equity Sales,
Maybank Kim Eng Securities Pte Ltd

"Stand on the shoulder of Mano – a giant among Singapore investors – and see it through his lens. You will see further by learning from the guru himself. Enjoy and share the learning from this book!"

— Seah Chye Ann
Former educator

MANO SABNANI'S

MONEY SECRETS

CRUISE YOUR WAY TO FINANCIAL FREEDOM

mc Marshall Cavendish
Business

© 2018 Mano Sabnani and Marshall Cavendish International (Asia) Pte Ltd

Reprinted 2018

Published in 2018 by Marshall Cavendish Business
An imprint of Marshall Cavendish International

A member of the
Times Publishing Group

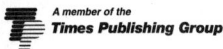

Other Marshall Cavendish Offices:
Marshall Cavendish Corporation. 99 White Plains Road, Tarrytown NY 10591–9001,
USA • Marshall Cavendish International (Thailand) Co Ltd. 253 Asoke, 12th Flr,
Sukhumvit 21 Road, Klongtoey Nua, Wattana, Bangkok 10110, Thailand • Marshall
Cavendish (Malaysia) Sdn Bhd, Times Subang, Lot 46, Subang Hi-Tech Industrial Park,
Batu Tiga, 40000 Shah Alam, Selangor Darul Ehsan, Malaysia.

Marshall Cavendish is a registered trademark of Times Publishing Limited

National Library Board, Singapore Cataloguing-in-Publication Data

Name(s): Sabnani, Mano.
Title: Mano Sabnani's money $ecrets : cruise your way to financial freedom.
Other title(s): Mano Sabnani's money secrets : cruise your way to financial freedom. |
Money $ecrets : cruise your way to financial freedom.
Description: Singapore : Marshall Cavendish Business, 2018.
Identifier(s): OCN 1045638494 | ISBN 978-981-4828-75-8 (paperback)
Subject(s): LCSH: Finance, Personal. | Investments. | Retirement—Planning.
Classification: DDC 332.024—dc23

Printed in Singapore

Cover and illustrations by Cheng Puay Koon

I hope this book leads to financial freedom and lasting happiness for you and your loved ones.

CONTENTS

FOREWORD

I am happy to write a short foreword for this book by Mano Sabnani, whom I have known since 1977 and regarded as a good friend ever since. But friendship is not the only reason I have agreed, without much hesitation, to take pen to paper (an old-fashioned expression that, doubtless, dates me). More important, it is the thought of helping to spread the word about how to attain financial security and freedom that I find hard to resist.

Mano could not have chosen a better time to release this book than now. Like it or not, Singapore is sliding inexorably into a phase in which job security is under relentless assault from every which quarter – disruptive technology, robotics, fund managers who pressure companies to report ever increasing returns on investment by squeezing workers, you name it. Many companies pay lip service to the mantra about valuing loyal and dedicated workers but have no qualms about letting them go when they are seen as a drag on the bottom line. Sad, yes, but that's reality today.

This is why Mano's words about the plight of corporate 'slaves' resonate with me – and, I suspect, all those who grit their teeth and swallow their pride no matter what unfairness or humiliation they encounter in the work place because they have mouths to feed and need desperately to keep their jobs. I have seen plenty of such cases in my forty-nine years of working life.

No doubt those still in employment, or even the ones out of it, should learn new skills and upgrade themselves. That is the familiar refrain from those securely at the top. I do not belittle the need for constant learning and education in this uncertain and somewhat scary age. I would argue, however, that it is also imperative that wage earners start planning and striving for financial security and freedom.

Here is where Mano's book will be a useful guide. To be sure, there must be plenty of investment guidebooks out there in the market. But this one is by someone who has immersed himself in the world of business and finance and investment for well over four decades and has the expertise honed over many years as a journalist to put thoughts and concepts across in jargon-free language. And above all else, he has himself attained financial freedom, which is about as convincing a calling card as you can get.

He knows what works here and what does not, and has been methodical in guiding his readers through all the potential pitfalls and hazards along the path to the financial freedom which he now wishes others to attain as well.

Happy reading!

Leslie Fong

Leslie Fong was *Straits Times* Editor from 1987 to 2002, the youngest at age thirty-seven to assume the post after joining the paper in late 1969. From journalism, he went on to head marketing and digital businesses for Singapore Press Holdings until his retirement in January 2016. He now sits on the board of two SPH subsidiaries and contributes comment and analysis pieces on East Asia periodically to the ST and *South China Morning Post.*

FOREWORD

In a room full of shareholders, one gentleman stood up to take the microphone. He shared a joke, which sent the crowd into loud laughter. What followed was more serious though: a word of thanks to the Board and management, a few deep and insightful comments, along with a question (or two) pertinent to the long-term success of Boustead Singapore.

The gentleman was none other than Mano Sabnani, whom I have had the honour of knowing for more than a decade, through our regular interactions at every one of our annual general meetings.

You can tell that he was well advised, having not only read the annual reports but also in the way that he was asking his questions – politely, but aiming to get the Board to share something meaningful, not just for him but also for every shareholder who was spending precious time to attend.

I am thankful that we have shareholders like Mano who decide that such meetings should be fruitful and perceptive affairs, rather than dull and procedural.

When Mano shared that he was writing this book on how anyone can attain financial freedom, it resonated with me. Having been born into a family of rubber tappers (we were not the plantation owners, mind you) in Malaysia, I grew up in poverty to the point that my family could barely make ends meet.

Among my siblings, I was the one focused on education, even learning English on my own, and graduated in chemical engineering from the University of New South Wales. Education gave me a good start and foundation. However, not satisfied with working for Exxon and Parsons early on even though the income was good, I eventually started my own businesses with a few successes and later ran several SGX-listed corporations as well.

Even at the age of 74, I have not retired. It is not because I have to work. I just have the financial freedom to choose what I would like to do with my time.

I would like the same for you as well. I believe that what Mano is proposing and sharing here may well lead you – with determination, education and hard work, along with a disciplined approach – to your financial freedom.

Wong Fong Fui

Wong Fong Fui is Chairman and Group CEO, Boustead Singapore group. He successfully turned around food manufacturing and retail company QAF Ltd as Group MD. He was also instrumental in the start-up and privatisation of Myanmar Airways International. An entrepreneur with proven success in diverse fields including education, information technology and telecommunications, Mr Wong was named Best Chief Executive Officer at the Singapore Corporate Awards.

PREFACE

Financial literacy and its promotion has been a subject close to my heart for a long time. I could say it goes back to the days when I started work as a young journalist in the *Business Times* (BT), a daily newspaper in Singapore. That was in 1977, and I hope my reports and commentaries helped investors to understand the economy and markets better.

Over the years, as I improved and built upon my own knowledge of business and the markets, I shared what I learned with the readers of BT. As I progressed to the role of chief editor in 1986, the paper took on a more active role in educating investors via its 'Personal Investment' section and other commentary and advisory columns.

At the *TODAY* newspaper where I was editor-in-chief and CEO from 2003 to 2006, I built up the business and investment section and wrote my own column as well as maintained a weekly appearance on TV in a segment called 'Today with Mano'. Since then, as CEO of financial and corporate consultancy Rafflesia Holdings, I have remained active as a writer and commentator in the newspapers and on radio as well as social media, including Facebook.

It is therefore only natural that I put my core ideas and views on investment and financial planning in a book. The objective of *Mano Sabnani's Money Secrets* is to promote financial literacy and to motivate and guide ordinary people to not only plan for their retirement, but to actively work towards attaining financial independence for themselves and their families.

I have taken a practical approach in the book and used simple language to put ideas across clearly and succinctly, so that anyone with a decent command of the English language can read and understand it easily, and follow up on the ideas. Readers can also draw inspiration from the fact that the author has actually followed the same plan and reached the goal of financial independence. Their circumstances may be different but the book explains how anyone can get to the same objective with discipline and persistence.

The past year has been as good a time as any for me to work on this book. I am now over sixty years of age and have written my autobiography *Marbles, Mayhem and my Typewriter*, which hit the bookshelves in December 2017. I have been motivated in the past ten months to work on *Money Secrets* by many of my friends and supporters. In particular, those who have read *Marbles* have asked that I write a book focused on investments and related subjects. So here it is, covering all the subjects that I am immersed in and which my readers have followed me on for some decades as a financial writer.

There are a total of nine chapters as well as a Prologue and an Epilogue, with one topic leading seamlessly to another. Feedback from readers will be most welcome. You can reach me at mano.sabnani@gmail.com. I am also active on Facebook with a blog called Manologue and a closed group called "Soul of Singapore" (anyone can apply to join) besides my personal profile. Manologue has over 800,000 followers while SoS has nearly 9,000 members who discuss a whole range of topics.

I have enjoyed writing the book and hope you find it useful and enjoyable. It could turn out to be a very rewarding investment if it helps you attain financial independence before the age of sixty, as I did. That objective will bring you and your family closer to lasting happiness.

My thanks are due to all the people who have inspired me to write the book and assisted the process in some way or other. In particular, I am deeply grateful to Steven Ooi, a good friend who has done volumes in researching the various topics and helping me in the draft stages of the manuscript. My appreciation also goes to my publisher, Marshall Cavendish International, who supported my efforts again in this second book.

I am very appreciative also of the friends and mentors who have contributed Forewords or reviews for the book and its covers. They have spent valuable time reading the manuscript and offering valuable feedback and comment.

Kindly note that all dollar amounts in this book refer to Singapore dollars unless otherwise specified. Also, there are times when I use only a 'he' or 'she' in human examples as it would be tedious to constantly refer to both genders. But the examples apply to both men and women.

Please also note that the contents of this book do not constitute financial advice to you as everyone's financial situation, personal objectives and individual needs are different. I am presenting only my own opinion and personal financial principles. You should do your own due diligence on all financial decisions and where necessary, consult a professional advisor. While every effort has been made to verify the facts stated in this book, no guarantee is made as to their accuracy.

Finally, the dedications. This book is dedicated to the many friends I have made in the course of my life's journey, in particular investors and corporate executives whom I have interacted with over the years. I have learnt much from them on the realities of business and investment. *Money Secrets* is also dedicated to my immediate family who have stood by me in this labour of love.

Lastly, but not least, the book is dedicated to you, my dear reader. Thank you for your interest and support. Enjoy the book and I hope it leads you to a better, more secure and happy life!

Mano Sabnani
August 2018

SLAVES IN A GLOBALISED WORLD

GLOBALISATION IS HERE TO STAY

Donald Trump thundered his way to the White House, Nigel Farage barraged the United Kingdom out of the European Union, and a host of far-right nationalist parties gained traction in Europe. In spite of all these, events thereafter strongly suggest that the trend towards globalisation is entrenched and irreversible. For the most part, borders have not slammed shut, nor trade wars erupted apart from some significant friction created by the Trump administration.

Companies, big and small, need to produce goods and services as efficiently as possible. Other than automation, they need the lowest cost of labour. So factories and service centres for a whole range of industries have been streaming into countries where the cost of labour is lower. Invariably, these are the less developed countries with large populations.

It helps if the countries are friendly to business and offer relatively low tax rates. Even better if the workforce is educated and trained in various skills and has positive work attitudes. China has been a big beneficiary for the last thirty years, so much so that it has evolved into the factory of the world.

Countries like Indonesia, Mexico, Vietnam and the Philippines have also benefited from the steady inflow of multinational companies (MNCs) seeking to lower their costs of production. Their relative political stability and pro-business policies have been helpful. Also important has been the business ecosystem where local companies sprout up everywhere to support the larger manufacturing and services companies from the United States, Germany, Japan and elsewhere.

There is no doubt that this flow of capital and knowledge to where labour costs are lowest has been beneficial to both the companies and the countries involved. Companies like Apple and Adidas have been able to stay highly competitive in their respective industries by producing quality goods at the best possible prices on a global scale. The countries where their products are made have gained from foreign investment inflows and steady take-up of their surplus labour.

CASUALTIES OF GLOBALISATION

But the global hunt for the lowest cost of labour has its losers. Employees inevitably become casualties when their jobs vanish in their home country. As companies reduce activity in high-labour-cost countries, they invariably shed workers and jobs. A few high-skilled jobs may be retained for research or design of products, but the bulk are moved out to the low-cost countries. The former employees of the MNCs could be considered losers.

While Chinese, Vietnamese, Mexican and Indonesian workers gain access to new jobs, their counterparts in the United States, Japan and Germany could be left adrift. As these trends entrench and spread themselves all over the world, there will be net winners and losers. I simplify. But the truth is that the workers with jobs gain while the jobless lose out in terms of quality of life. Social safety nets help, but there is a limit to what they can do.

Hence, the rising unpopularity of the globalisation trend in many countries. Any casual observer will note that the greater unhappiness is in the developed countries of the European Union and the United States. The hollowing out of the manufacturing bases of these countries has taken place over the last two or three decades and has now reached critical proportions. Whole communities and towns are feeling the effects more acutely.

CREATING WIN-WIN SITUATIONS

However, there is a solution to this ostensibly unacceptable situation where low-cost countries gain in jobs and incomes seemingly at the expense of the more developed countries.

Education, training and continuous learning are key to creating win-win situations for all. The same workers can be made useful in new vocations or professions. But this requires a pro-active government, firms, unions, and/or community organisations anticipating trends and preparing for the changes. They have to anticipate the movement of certain economic activities out of their domestic bases due to dwindling competitiveness. Companies alone cannot be expected to take up the burden of keeping workers employable or looking after those made redundant when manufacturing activity is shifted elsewhere.

All have to work together to re-train workers in advance for more sophisticated jobs which will be retained or in demand in their more developed economies. This is where countries like

Denmark and Germany have succeeded and the United States has failed.

Denmark has a much-lauded system known as "flexicurity", with three components: (1) labour market flexibility, (2) generous benefits and (3) extensive active labour market policies – in particular education and training – to get people back to work[1]. Unemployed Danes receive as much as 90 percent of their previous wage (for low-skilled workers), but a condition of receiving this benefit is attendance in 'activation' programmes, notably training.

The classroom education approach in Denmark is highly flexible with an average course duration of only three-and-a-half days but with more than 2,800 courses on offer. These are constantly updated to match the skills sought by employers. This allows participants to customise their selection to their needs. The unemployed are entitled to six weeks of education free of charge but those who are employed also use the training with significant public support. Hiring and firing can happen at any time, which gives Danish companies a distinct advantage over many other European states. But workers have a great chance of finding another job fairly quickly, as the system takes care of them while they prepare and search for their next job. According to Eurostat, unemployment was 4.9 percent in Mar 2018, which compares very favourably with the European Union average of 7.1 percent. In short, flexicurity promotes employment security over job security.

The United States, under the Donald Trump presidency, is attempting to entice companies to retain relatively low-skilled jobs in the country instead of moving them across the border to Mexico or elsewhere such as to Vietnam and China. This effort is likely to have very limited success unless the whole question of total cost of producing the various goods is examined and the companies are assisted with various other incentives so that producing those goods in the United States makes sense.

The alternative is for the United States to work harder on its education system to ensure graduates from its colleges and universities have the requisite skills to take up jobs in relatively new industries that are growing rapidly. It should not be necessary for fast-growing companies in Silicon Valley, for example, to hire large numbers of IT and other professionals from overseas. Americans should be ready to take up these vacancies.

Globalisation could be a win-win for all countries if people acquire the pertinent skills to take up the better-paying jobs that are being created in their respective countries. But this is easier said than done. Political will is lacking in many countries and so the seeming negative effects of globalisation can be played up to the benefit of no one.

HOW TO BE A WINNER IN A GLOBALISED WORLD

My focal point, however, in this prologue is that in the globalised world, *it is the entrepreneurs and investors who are the real long-term winners.*

Talent can flow anywhere and cheap labour from another country can keep wages down at home, artificially. While the foreign labour or workers from less well-off countries benefit by moving overseas to work, the resident or citizen workers in industrialised nations see a flat trend in their wages. But even the migrant workers as well as their countrymen back home working at the factory in Bac Ninh, Vietnam, or the call centre in Iloilo City, the Philippines, see only a limited benefit as, after all, their appeal to the MNCs is that they are cheap. Their wages can never rise beyond a certain point, and while they may enjoy a higher standard of living than most of their countrymen, most will still not be able to afford an iPhone or a nice house in a good location.

Multiply this pattern across the globe and what we have is stagnation or even the gradual diminution of real wages, or wages after factoring in inflation. Workers in poorer countries with fast-growing populations keep down wages of workers in richer countries. It is either the workers move to higher-wage locations or jobs move to where wages are lowest.

The winners are companies which can relocate to where wages are low or stay at home and employ large numbers of cheap foreign workers and executives. The MNCs have myriad factors to consider to ensure their competitiveness and survival. So no one should begrudge them their nimble decisiveness in locating their operations where it best suits them.

But stagnant wages for the vast majority of workers for the same job done means there is little to no wealth being built and no cushion available for the future and for retirement. It means that unless a worker rises to top management level in a company or possesses a skill that is in severe shortage, such as Artificial Intelligence engineering, he or she will be stuck in a rut for the best years of his or her life.

Such workers will not have enough savings for a comfortable retirement, or even to retire at all (the sad sight of many elderly folks still operating a pedicab in the Philippines or cleaning tables at hawker centres in Singapore bears testament). Many will live from hand to mouth in their supposed 'golden years' as inflation mercilessly gobbles up any small increments attained over the years. A tragic outcome for people who followed mummy and daddy's advice to work hard their entire lives, only to find that it never brought them the security or good life that was promised.

At the end of the day, entrepreneurship and investing are the two best tools to ensure you do not become a slave in a globalised world dominated by MNCs.

Entrepreneurship

Wage earners can work towards being their own bosses at some stage of their working lives. Entrepreneurship is a tough grind but it can ultimately be very rewarding. Owning a profitable company with strong competitive advantages and sound financing is an excellent way to ensure financial independence for you and your family for a long time to come.

A Savings And Investment Plan

The other way out of this wage trap is to *scrape, save and invest while one is a wage earner.* A disciplined, regular savings and investment plan can help millions of wage earners to get out of the wage trap and build up enough reserves for retirement. This book deals with that. The ultimate aim is financial independence or freedom, which means wage income is no longer necessary to maintain your lifestyle indefinitely.

If wage earners don't work on their retirement plans from a young age, they will end up as slaves to MNCs in a globalised world. The same applies to workers in the public sector or government. Their real wages are also destined to be flat over the years, unless they are exceptional performers who move up the ranks or switch jobs midstream with newly acquired skills and aptitudes.

But greed reigns in a capitalist world, and the financial markets are a sea of sharks out to feast on the naive or uninformed. Numerous unregulated 'investment' schemes also turn out to be scams. How can ordinary folks avoid the deceptions and pitfalls, and invest profitably? I shall deal with this in later chapters – read on.

---

1 "Flexicurity", The Official Website of Denmark http://denmark.dk/en/society/welfare/flexicurity

CHAPTER 1

ARE YOU FINANCIALLY LITERATE?

Education systems everywhere teach subjects like mathematics, language, history, geography, science, literature and specialised skills like technical drawing, metalwork and even art.

But few schools anywhere in the world teach their students financial literacy – a core life skill that equips them with the knowledge and skills to make good financial decisions in life. For example, what do you do with money that comes your way through work or business or as a gift from your parents or other benefactors? Do you simply spend it on the things you need or want to own? How do you assess the value of the item or service you are prepared to pay for?

Do you sometimes feel that you have paid too much for something you bought? What do you do about it? Do you learn from the episode or do you soon forget it and go on to buy, some time later, similarly over-priced goods and services?

Before you commit to buying something, do you pause to assess whether you really need the item? Needing a new handbag or wallet is quite different from wanting it because it is a prestigious brand or because you simply like the looks of it. And if your assessment suggests you do not need the item, do you then drop the idea and keep the money aside?

The subject of financial literacy is not a complicated one and I intend to convey my thoughts and approaches to as many people as possible in as simple a way as possible. Some calculations of dollars and cents will be necessary, but we need not delve too deeply into mathematical concepts. This is because financial literacy is, above all, about attitude and personal discipline.

It has to do with how you view money and its purpose in life. Is money something only to be spent so as to own as much as possible and to enjoy goods and services? Is the purpose of money to give you a good life such as having as big a house as possible with many possessions in it; a big, expensive car and luxurious holidays and other pastimes?

Or is money something that helps you meet your basic needs of food, housing, transport, education and medical care? Do you recognise that putting aside some money for the future is a good habit or do you see it as dwindling in value over time?

Is money, to you, more a symbol of status and power, a source of security or something else? Perhaps it's even a means to help others?

These are important questions every thinking individual should ask himself or herself quietly. If you are prudent in spending money and acquire and keep only what you really need, then you are on the right track. Otherwise, you will need to change your approach to money first before you can develop financial literacy and embark on the road to financial independence and a healthy financial situation throughout your life.

THE THREE PRONGS OF FINANCIAL PLANNING

There are three main prongs of financial planning which can help you achieve your dream of financial freedom: savings, insurance and investment.

Work sedulously to build up these three areas and you will have a good chance of getting there. But it is easier said than done! To achieve your long-term financial goals, there is a need to be consistent, diligent and disciplined. Year-in and year-out, you will need to stick to your savings and investment plan.

"But I'm just not good with money," you might protest. "I just don't have the (a) interest, (b) patience, (c) discipline and/ or (d) time to do all this!"

I will address these common objections and reservations.

Your Worst Enemy Is Yourself

Benjamin Graham, widely known as "the father of value investing" and the mentor of world famous investor Warren Buffett, wrote in his seminal book *The Intelligent Investor*:

> "For indeed, the investor's chief problem – and even his worst enemy – is likely to be himself."

Paraphrasing Shakespeare, he goes on to say:

> "The fault, dear investor, is not in our stars – and not in our stocks – but in ourselves."

As imperfect human beings, there will surely be flaws in our nature that can hurt us in our financial decision-making. These flaws differ from person to person, and achieving financial success requires a good, hard look in the mirror. Some of us are prone to overspending to impress people; others may be lazy when it comes to doing research on investments and will buy stocks based only on a dubious 'hot tip'. Some fail to control their emotions and their greed drives them to buy a stock that has become grossly overpriced; yet others may be too egotistical to listen to different viewpoints on the merits of an investment.

What are *your* flaws in financial decision-making?

Whatever these may be, and whatever dreadful mistakes you have made in the past, rest assured that *with patience and dedication, you can improve yourself* and cultivate the right qualities to become financially liberated.

One of the most wonderful things I've discovered is that the journey of financial planning is also the journey of personal growth. Discipline, patience, critical thinking, the ability to make tough decisions while mastering emotions – these are all highly worthwhile personal qualities in every aspect of our lives.

The key is to keep at it, and never give up. Every time you fall, do not keep lamenting it but learn from it and come out stronger every time. Go to any coffee shop and you will hear an old man bemoaning a painful loss in Stock XYZ that he suffered twenty or even thirty years ago. *Don't dwell on your mistakes; learn from them.*

As you become a better financial decision-maker and investor, you also become a better person.

To those who say that they have no interest in the topic, you should ask yourself whether you have any interest in achieving financial security and having a comfortable retirement. If you have an interest in the ends, then you must *take* an interest in the means. Otherwise it basically means that you want to harvest the fruits, but don't want to learn how to plant the tree.

No time, you say? When you want something badly enough, you will *make* the time. Understandably, we are all busy people. But many successful investors found ways to carve out bits of time from their schedules to learn the basics, keep up with business news and research companies. I know a high-flying corporate executive who does stock research during short breaks at work and checks out the assets of listed companies when he travels for work. Another friend juggled a seven-day work week and being a husband and father with investing. On some Saturday nights, he would dig out an hour to scour *The Edge* business weekly for opportunities.

If you will pardon my bluntness, losers make excuses. Winners make solutions.

And if you say you have "no time" to learn financial planning and investing now, you may well find that when you reach the age of fifty-five, sixty-five or even seventy-five, you will have "no time" for your children, your spouse, yourself. Because you will still be working out of necessity, slogging day to day, living from pay cheque to pay cheque.

The two friends I mentioned achieved financial freedom at age forty and forty-two respectively. Yet another friend did it at thirty-two. All three are family men with children to support.

And now they can spend as much time as they want with their loved ones and pursuing their personal interests.

There will of course be unexpected events which can set you back in certain periods. That is life, isn't it? It is not always smooth sailing. One has to be as prepared as possible for ups and downs. So a good financial plan provides for setbacks and variation in the rate of return on investments. A good plan is also customised to the person or family it is for. You can seek external advice on the details but *it is important to know what you want and how you can go about it.*

Prong No. 1: Savings

As with all things in life, begin with Common Sense. It's become a tired old joke by now that Common Sense is most uncommon. Why it is so is open to debate – perhaps as the world grows increasingly complex, people forget their basics. Perhaps we sometimes allow nonsense ideas and beliefs to become entrenched in our minds simply because everyone else buys into them. But whatever the case, when we fail to exercise Common Sense in our financial decisions, the results are not at all funny.

So here is Common Sense Rule No. 1 in building your financial future: *You must spend less than you earn.* As self-made millionaire and financial advisor Guy Baker puts it, money does not fall from the sky. Nothing will happen unless you first save money.[1]

Sadly, the sight of many elderly people in the queue for lottery tickets in Singapore suggests that far too many people have not grasped this most basic principle even by the age of eighty. They are still hoping for a windfall from the gods. The chances are so remote (one out of a million or less) that one might have to live through a hundred lifetimes before one strikes that elusive jackpot. And if one has not learned the principles of personal financial management, those millions of dollars are likely to evaporate in just a few years anyway.

So, spend less than you earn. You might be surprised that this can be more difficult for high earners than those earning less, because when you make $25,000 a month, your expectations (and others' expectations of you) will probably also be much higher than for a guy making $4,000. But whether it's $25,000 or $1,500, you must find a way to shape your lifestyle to fit below your means. This means real sacrifice and tough trade-offs.

For me, personally, the habit of saving was inculcated by my parents from a young age. My two elder siblings and younger sister and brothers all had piggy banks. We were encouraged to save some of our pocket money for future needs. I thus learnt to squirrel away coins in my primary school days. Thirty cents was all I got each day for pocket money, of which ten cents was for bus fare and twenty cents for food and drink at recess.

Of course, things cost much less in the late 1950s and early 1960s, but it was still hard to save. Saving ten cents a day meant eating a curry puff instead of a plate of noodles during school recess; and drinking water from the tap instead of a five-cents ready-made drink of soya bean milk or syrup.

The government also encouraged the savings habit in those days and we had the Post Office Savings Bank (POSB) van visiting schools once a fortnight to encourage students to save. We bought stamps with our savings and these were then stuck in a brown album. When the album was full, it meant we had saved a few dollars. These were then handed over to the POSB officer and our savings passbook would be updated. Everything was done manually in those days as computers were unheard of.

But that saving habit stuck for life. In secondary school, I continued to painstakingly build up my savings in POSB which has long since gone its own way, having built itself up as a formidable people's savings bank by the 1980s.

My very first bank account was with POSB and that account remains with me today, after more than fifty years! Of course, things have changed now. POSB is a part of DBS or the Development Bank of Singapore group.

Under DBS, it appears that POSB is also more profit-oriented and trying to make its deposits work harder for a return. That has allowed the DBS group to grow rapidly and reward its shareholders well.

But the POSB's legions of depositors, like those of other banks in Singapore, receive a very poor return on their savings. Savings accounts hardly yield anything even over a year while fixed deposits (FDs) of one-year duration yield less than 1 percent. Like other commercial banks, DBS has as its core objective a need to maintain a healthy interest margin between its loans and deposits.

The point I am making here is that saving some of your earnings or allowances in a bank is still a good habit or practice. You are building for the future, but the low rate of return means your savings may actually be eroded or gradually lose their value due to effects of inflation. This is why you need to learn how to *invest* those savings, but certainly saving is the first step.

Inflation, even in countries that enjoy price stability like Singapore, is still hovering at around 2 percent or more. It all depends on how you measure inflation and which goods and services are taken into account. In Singapore from 1990 to 2000, the consumer price index (CPI) inflation was 1.7 percent annually; from 2000 to 2010, 1.6 percent; from 2010 to 2017, 1.8 percent[2]. For the entire span of twenty-seven years, inflation averaged 1.7 percent. So if you're not earning anything close to

1 percent on your Singapore dollar deposits in banks, then you are really allowing your savings to erode steadily.

We will discuss the topic of banks and why they are not really your friend, in another chapter of this book. For now, it is sufficient to say that financial literacy means not only developing the right attitude towards money and having a savings habit; it means you have to invest at least some of your savings for higher returns.

First, you have to keep aside a percentage of your daily or monthly income as savings. It would be even better if you can work out what you need as expenses each month and set that aside in a household or personal expenses account. Your expenses can then all be drawn from this account.

The other bank account should be where your salary or business income goes into; this should be your savings and investment account. It is important to separate the accounts so you can monitor easily the progress of your financial plan. Every now and then, but at least once in six months, you should sit down and examine the state of your two accounts: their inflows and outflows and the state of your cash balances and investments.

As your savings accumulate, you should work on your financial literacy. There is no shortage of good books, newspaper articles and websites on various subjects like stocks and shares, property, bonds and other fixed income instruments; and even antiques and art. But before you plunge into any of these instruments, do make a financial plan for yourself and the family.

A financial plan is the big picture of your family's situation and how it is likely to progress in the future. It takes into account your sources of income, your regular expenses and any commitments you may have in terms of loan repayments or education for the children. The savings picture is then clearer and insurance policies can be purchased and investments made accordingly.

A cardinal rule is that one should always keep enough cash to sustain oneself and any dependants for at least six months. This can be called an emergency fund and it provides for situations where the regular cash inflow dries up for whatever reason – such as job loss. Many people ignore or forget this 'commandment', probably because it is so thoroughly boring (unlike the prospect of sexy profits in stocks). But if you ignore the boring principles, you will not achieve exciting returns in life. *Without the buffer of a cash reserve, you may well be caught defenceless in an emergency, and be forced to sell your investments at the worst possible time* like during the 2008 global financial crisis, when many good stocks crashed 50 percent or more.

At this point you may be very eager to learn about investing, but before that...

Prong No. 2: Insurance

Before we think about investing our savings to grow our wealth (akin to building a football team's offence), we need first to build our defence. We need to protect ourselves and our families against catastrophic events, especially during our economically productive years as such events could seriously impair our ability to build our financial future. I am talking about the unpropitious possibilities that may befall any of us mere mortals, like death, serious illness, and fire.

It may not be possible to raise enough cash from investments when the unfortunate happens. Insurance should be there to cover such exigencies, so that the financial plan can proceed without too much disruption.

This book will cover life insurance and health insurance. I urge you to also find out more about other forms of protection that may be relevant to you, such as fire insurance if you are a home owner.

Your financial planner or insurance agent or broker should be able to advise you on the insurance policies best suited to you or your family.

Life insurance

Life insurance protects against financial loss that would ensue in the event of a person's death. Upon the demise of the insured, the insurance company pays a sum of money to the beneficiaries named by the insured. Most such policies also give the insured the option to receive – at additional cost – a payout in the events of total and permanent disability, and dread illnesses such as cancer and kidney failure.

There are broadly two types of life insurance – participating and non-participating. The former gives the policyholder the right to receive a portion of the investment returns achieved by the insurer using the premiums paid by the policyholder. The latter does not.

Non-participating policies provide you higher dollar coverage for each dollar of premium paid. They usually come in the form of term policies which cover you for only a fixed period, say up to the age of sixty. At that age they expire and offer no cash returns at the end point.

It is important to note that once the policy expires, it no longer offers any protection. Should the untoward happen after that point, the erstwhile policyholder or his beneficiaries would not receive any payout unless he also has a participating policy.

On the other hand, participating life policies with benefits or profit-sharing require premiums to be paid to a ripe old age and provide you less protection per dollar paid, but they build up cash values over time so that you have the option of terminating the policies and pocketing the cash value, or using the cash to pay for premiums at an advanced age. Today many participating policies are investment-linked, and a percentage of your premiums will be invested in mutual funds (also known as unit trusts). If you purchase such a policy, you will be asked to make a choice of what proportion of your premium you wish to allocate to which mutual fund. It is important to educate yourself on the risks and potential returns from the different kinds of mutual funds before you make your choice.

The amount of payout when a claim occurs will depend to a considerable extent on the performance of the investments linked to one's policy.

For me, personally, my family has been provided for with a mix of participating and non-participating policies. The latter (term policies) are for larger amounts and some are linked to SAFRA (Singapore Armed Forces Reservist Association) and the Automobile Association of Singapore. These group policies are handled by the insurance companies for these organisations and come at a low cost due to the large base of insured persons.

Health insurance

Health insurance covers the cost of an individual's hospitalisation and surgery (H & S). This can be paid for by the state, the employer and/or the individual in varying proportions.

We should note the specific types of hospitalisation, surgical and medical procedures that are covered by the policy and the maximum disbursements provided for each. We also need to note the deductible – any H & S expenses below this level in a given year will not be covered – and the co-payment, which is the percentage of the expenses (after subtracting the deductible) which will have to be borne by the insured.

Bear in mind also that health insurance is expensive and difficult to sustain over the long term as premiums can be raised over time. In Singapore, the government has promoted MediShield Life which allows for premiums to be paid via Central Provident Fund (CPF) savings. This is a good way to go. You can enhance the coverage through integrated plans which basically involve private insurers building on the MediShield coverage if you are willing to pay additional premiums.

MediShield Life operates on the basis that a hospital bill is shared between the scheme, your own MediSave savings and some cash payout on your part. The government also provides subsidies of varying amounts based on the individual's age, financial situation and capacity to pay. Most Singaporeans have relied on this package to provide cover for their families. Some have integrated plans.

These insurance policies are for the long term. Maximum benefits are usually derived when you retain the policies to full maturity. Bear in mind that you and your family usually lose out if or when you terminate policies prematurely. It costs more to enter into policies at a later age and even more when you have pre-existing medical conditions. So commit to policies for yourself and the family as early as possible. Work out the annual premiums and ensure you are able to sustain the payments through the years.

Tied agents vs independent advisors

Currently in Singapore and some other countries, insurance can be purchased either from agents tied to a particular insurance company, or independent advisors. The advantage of the latter is that they can recommend to you policies from a range of insurers instead of only one – thus, assuming they are honest, they will be better able to recommend a policy that best suits your needs. Another advantage of independent advisors is that they typically charge you advisory fees rather than commissions.

As their fees are usually less than the commissions paid to them by the insurers, they give you a periodic refund amounting to the commissions minus their fees.

An important caveat

At this point, let us consult our Common Sense once more. What does it tell us? That not everyone can be trusted and, likewise, not every insurance company or independent advisor can be trusted.

Thus, before you make a major commitment to take up an insurance policy which you will need to pump tens of thousands of dollars into over the years, *do your research on that insurance company or advisor.* Read the news and see if there have been any reports of unsavoury actions by them, or financial troubles. Speak to friends and family who have had lengthy experiences dealing with them, especially in the all-important area of claims. Does the company treat its policyholders well and try its best to pay a claim? Or does it try its best to avoid paying by banking on little technicalities? When one needs some service or queries answered after one buys the policy, does the company provide prompt and attentive service? Does it treat its staff fairly? There are many clues as to what an insurance company or advisory firm is made of, ethically.

Do not assume that an organisation is honest and principled just because it is well known or large.

Beware also of unprincipled insurance agents. There have been cases of agents committing fraud.

Prong No. 3: Investment

When bank deposit interest rates are lower than the rate of inflation, the value of your cash savings contracts over time at a compound rate. As mentioned earlier, inflation has averaged about 1.7 percent in the last three decades or so. If this rate continues into the future, your $4 plate of chicken rice in 2018 will set you back by $4.90 in 2030 and $5.80 in 2040.

Bear in mind that inflation has a compounding effect – the additional 1.7 cents added to each dollar of price in one year will itself grow by 1.7 percent (to 1.73 cents) in the following year, and 1.76 cents in the next and so on. Thus the increase in prices after ten years is not 1.7 percent times 10 (17 percent), but 18.4 percent. After twenty years, the price increase is not 34 percent, but 40.1 percent.

At the time of writing in 2018, a savings account with a local bank pays you only 0.05–0.1 percent (it can rise to 0.8 percent annualised, but only if certain conditions are met, such as no withdrawals in a given month and a larger initial deposit) while a 12-month Singapore dollar fixed or time deposit pays only about 0.5 percent (around 1.2 percent during promotional offers). Even if one gets the 1.2 percent rate and is able to roll over interest and principal at the same rate to compound returns for twelve years and twenty-two years respectively, $4 would only grow to $4.62 in 2030 and $5.20 in 2040. You would still be short of 28 cents and 60 cents respectively when ordering that plate of chicken rice!

Investing and trading: know the difference

First, let us draw a crucial distinction between investing and trading. Trading is trying to get in and out of an asset fast, trying to ride the ebb and flow of the market to one's own advantage. Thus traders study the patterns of price movement and use them to try to extrapolate the future – in the case of stock trading, the players use technical analysis: a rather esoteric methodology of charts showing price movements, volume changes and an array of associated mathematical calculations and visual patterns. A trader buys a stock because he believes the price is going to go up fairly soon.

Investing, on the other hand, is about paying 50 cents or 60 cents for an asset that one believes is worth a dollar (this is known as *intrinsic value*, the objective worth of the stock based on the profitability, balance sheet strength and corporate governance of the company). The investor generally has a long-term horizon: she is prepared, and indeed often expects, to wait for years before she realises her desired gains. Thus an investor buys a stock because she believes the current price is far below what it is objectively and intrinsically worth, and at some point the gap between value and price will narrow.

It is possible to succeed as an investor or trader, but I believe it is much better to be an investor. My reasons are:

(a) Investing does not require very close daily monitoring of the market. As long as you have a strong conviction that the stock or company is undervalued based on highly probable prospects for its business, you can just update yourself on company results once a quarter and other announcements perhaps once a month just to make sure that your investment thesis remains on track. Warren Buffett is well known for hardly checking the prices of his stock holdings – he is more focused on the news about the business, because he believes that despite all the temperamental short-term gyrations of the market, the fundamentals of the business are the strongest drivers of the stock price in the long term.

(b) Investing is considerably less stressful than trading. True investors are not much perturbed by a 20 percent fall in their stock price in the short term (of course it would be hard for any human being not to be perturbed by a 50 percent fall, but the investor would be much less troubled than a trader). This is because an investor engages in assets based on intrinsic value and knows that despite short-term slumps in share price based on crowd emotions or traumatic world events such as a financial crisis, terror attack or pandemic, the share price will gravitate back towards its intrinsic value once the world normalises.

(c) Investment is based on sounder scientific principles than trading. *Technical analysis may appear to be highly scientific and be anchored in scientific certainty; in reality it is anything but.* The chart pattern that showed tremendous momentum and a moving average convergence-divergence (MACD – a popular indicator used by traders) line rising above the signal line may not reflect genuine market sentiment or direction at all – it could simply have been manipulated by a group of people with deep pockets. When they pull their money out of the market, the price (and your chart formulas) will collapse spectacularly. Likewise if some fundamental weakness in the company comes to light, for instance a revelation of accounting irregularities, or there is an outbreak of a terrible disease like SARS.

Investing is based on much firmer, more objective rational concepts (which I describe as 'scientific') such as profit margin, net cash or net debt, free cashflow and so on. Even if a terrible pandemic breaks out tomorrow, it does not mean that the cash on a company's balance sheet is no longer real. This is why I believe that investing offers us a more reliable way to make money than trading does. It is based on *fundamentals*, and is therefore *fundamentally* sound. You get to grow financially with the growth of a business, with steady increases in portfolio value.

A comparison between the two men widely regarded as the greatest investor who ever lived – Warren Buffett – and the greatest trader who ever lived – Jesse Livermore – provides rich food for thought. Livermore – who was worth US\$100 m at his peak in 1929, the equivalent of an estimated US\$1.7 b in today's dollars – went broke numerous times, divorced twice, had a stream of mistresses and committed suicide in 1940. His first divorce was in no small part triggered by his losing everything in the market and demanding that his wife pawn the jewellery he had given her. According to Tom Rubython in his book *Jesse Livermore – Boy Plunger: The Man Who Sold America Short in 1929* (The Myrtle Press, 2015), his third wife's US$7 m fortune had lulled him into a sense of comfort and killed the desperation to win he had in his youth. He felt as if he was losing himself.

Buffett, on the other hand, has had a far more steady career in the stock market to become the third richest person on the Earth[3] with a net worth of US$75.6 b (despite giving away vast amounts to charity). He was worth about US$1.4 m in 1962 (at age thirty-two), US$620 m in 1983 and became a billionaire in 1986. He has also enjoyed a much more stable personal life, though he was separated from his first wife till her death and is now married to his second. He is still hale and hearty at the ripe old age of eighty-eight.

Of course I would hesitate to draw generalisations about traders and investors based solely on these two prominent individuals. But it makes sense to me that an investing *mindset*, with its emphasis on fundamentals and long-term development, is much more likely to produce a fulfilling and stable personal life as well. It is better to treat life as a long-term investment than a series of quick trades and speedy gratifications.

Traders generate a lot more commissions for their brokers and fees for stock exchanges. That's why you can expect brokers and exchanges to promote trading more actively than investing. We also live in a very impatient world today, with people often expecting profits at fibre broadband speed. Will you be enticed by 'sexy methods' of achieving quick trading profits, or follow the boring, patient but proven approach of great investors like Warren Buffett, Benjamin Graham or Peter Lynch? It is up to you.

What to invest in, how to invest, and when to invest?

You can read my principles of investing and best strategies for the long term in Chapter 5.

---

1 "Getting rich systematically", Kelvin Tan, *The Edge Singapore*, The Edge Publishing Pte Ltd. 23 May 2005

2 Calculated using CPI figures from Department of Statistics Singapore website, http://www.tablebuilder.singstat.gov.sg/publicfacing/createDataTable.action?refId=12005

3 Forbes 2017 Billionaires List: Meet the Richest People on the Planet, https://www.forbes.com/billionaires/#1dda96c6251c

CHAPTER 2

IS SGX THE SINGAPORE GAMBLING EXCHANGE?

You've heard people say it often. The stock market is a casino. There are those who stay away from it completely. They prefer to keep their money in the bank or in what they perceive to be safe bonds or in investment property. That is an option, of course. Those who keep their savings in banks enjoy some interest but it is more often than not lower than the rate of inflation in their own country. The result is that they suffer a gradual erosion in their savings with the banks as the main beneficiaries.

THE VOLATILITY OF STOCK MARKETS

The stock market is another option, but is it really safe to wade into its turbulent waters? Given the volatility, is it better to invest in them via third-party fund managers or even exchange-traded funds (ETFs), which follow indices up and down? The concern here is that individual stocks are even more volatile than the overall market and so perceived risks are higher.

If you venture directly into the markets with the right principles and discipline, you can do better than most fund managers and ETFs. You need to cut out the noise from daily traders and focus on the fundamentals of companies. Good companies will ride out the volatility of the market and emerge smelling like roses at the end of the day as their business grows and profits and reserves accumulate over the years.

It does happen that good companies, with strong business models and capable management, suffer during bad economic times or when bad taxation and other policies are introduced by inept governments. They will not do as well as expected but will probably still outperform many other companies in the same marketplace.

There can also be extreme volatility in the markets which makes it difficult for good companies to raise new capital via rights issues or placements to third parties. Their depressed share prices can also make it hard for the companies to borrow more from their regular bankers, no thanks to low market capitalisations. Owners of companies will find it hard to pledge their shares as collateral to raise new funds for business diversification.

The reality is that the stock market is an unpredictable place. Fortunes can rise and fall; wax and wane in the period of a few years. It can create an enormous amount of wealth over a short period, when the buyers or bulls are present in large numbers and show insatiable appetites. Many stock prices can go on a steep uptrend and the market's capitalisation can multiply and soar to great heights as seen in the 2007 bull market and earlier runs in the seventies, eighties and nineties. Each time a bull market rears its head, much wealth is created and it has effects on real life in various sectors. People feel good and spend more on a wide variety of consumer staples as well as on property and other investments.

Some get greedy and even carried away. As it is easy to make money in a bull market, people forget that it is sometimes not their own skill but the rising market that allows them to make easy money in the stock market. They over-invest, often on borrowed capital, in the hope of getting rich as quickly as possible. That is human nature and this weakness is exploited by big speculators who operate individually or in syndicates. Sometimes, the broking firms get involved as well, pushing certain stocks to ever-higher levels, using their own traders and capital.

Examples of such booms were seen in the mid-eighties when a few stocks in Singapore, led by Pan Electric, were pushed to huge valuations and unjustified prices. Trading syndicates and stockbroking firms were involved and when the music eventually stopped, as it must, the scramble to get out was not manageable. A few bad stocks falling steeply every day affected the whole market and eventually trading had to be called to a halt to sort out the mess, with the Monetary Authority of Singapore (MAS) involved.

The collapse of Pan Electric and its sister Growth Industrial Holdings, as well as certain Malaysian-based high-flyers such as Multi-Purpose Holdings and Malayan United Industries, led to the failure of a few stockbroking firms. It eventually resulted in a re-constitution of the Stock Exchange of Singapore (SES) from a member-based system to an ownership model (SGX), with the government taking a significant share via Temasek Holdings. Certain people were brought to book for their involvement in the creation of the untenable bubble led by Pan Electric.

Thus, the stock market is prone to extreme bubbles and the party can carry on for some time. But when the party comes to an end, as it has to for whatever reason, the fallout can be severe all round. Prices can fall and fall and values can shrink to a fraction of their peaks. Shenanigans can exploit investors to enrich their masterminds through dubious deals and corporate manoeuvres, especially in euphoric times. Stock exchange and company regulations cannot always stop them; every bull market throws up new situations.

The bear markets that follow bullish runs are a reversal of all the positive effects felt earlier. The pain is felt all round by investors and corporate chieftains. Bad news is the order of the day. As values keep falling, individual investors try to flee the market. Some stay put and become unwilling long-term investors! Fund manager portfolios are decimated as unit holders pull out, leading to a vicious cycle where low prices lead to even lower prices.

Bear markets also affect the real economy. Consumers spend less as the wealth effect dissipates; less consumables are bought and big ticket items are avoided, affecting companies dealing in properties and cars. The subdued environment on the ground eventually filters up to the profits of companies in a wide range of business and industry. The stock market can go down to the same level it started from for its bull leg, or even much lower.

I hear you asking whether it is possible to get out of this bull and bear cycle. Or is it possible to stop these cycles? My own view is that the cycles will continue: the uptrend, which leads to greed and excessive values, and then the downturn, with its uncontrolled fear, to realistic prices and finally bargain-basement prices. The cycle is part and parcel of the capitalist system and the markets.

Investors can actually benefit from the ups and downs in the stock and property markets. Keep cash handy at all times and when the downturn comes, you have to be ready to pick up cheap stock or property, or both, as you prefer. Good stocks can be bought at bargain-basement prices when the going is rough in the stock market.

THE DIFFERENCES BETWEEN STOCK MARKETS AND CASINOS; INVESTING AND GAMBLING

The stock market is, in reality, quite fundamentally different from a casino. It has a serious purpose – to raise funds for companies and allow them to expand their business with larger equity bases. If the companies do well, everyone gains: the employees and owners, including small shareholders. It is not a zero-sum game like the casino where either you win or the house wins. Both cannot be winners. Also, there are deep skills involved in studying companies and selecting stocks based on their business fundamentals and valuations. The same cannot be said of a casino punter.

But unfortunately, there are people who treat the stock market as a casino. They plunge into the market based on pure guesswork, 'gut feelings' with no fundamental basis, rumours, hot tips and other flimsy reasons. Sometimes they go into a stock simply because it is going up – which Warren Buffett called "the dumbest reason in the world to buy a stock".

What about those who use historical price and volume charts, as well as various patterns based on technical analysis? Well, such 'technically' grounded trading may be more 'scientific' than purely instinctive or random gambling, but there is a fine line between the two due to the rather tenuous and arbitrary nature of technical analysis as explained in Chapter 1 (see 'Investing and trading: know the difference').

Just as understanding the difference between investing and trading is crucial if you are to achieve financial liberation, so is a strong grasp of *the distinction between investing and gambling*. Investing is based on decisions made on a *sound, logical assessment of probabilities* whereas gambling involves *wild swings at the game of chance*. In other words, a proper investor puts money down when he logically believes the probabilities or odds are in his favour; a gambler puts money down without caring whether the odds are in his favour (in a casino, they are always in favour of the house) and just hopes it is his lucky day.

Both the gambler and investor can win or lose, but an investor who has done his homework properly has a much better chance of winning on any given decision, and over a lifetime of decisions, is almost certain to do better than the gambler. The gambler might get lucky once, twice, even three times but, eventually, the odds catch up with him and he will surrender all his winnings (and usually much more) to the house.

Stock gamblers and traders alike buy and sell frequently and in large quantities. Stockbrokers love them for the liquidity and commissions they generate, and they fuel both bull and bear markets. They win sometimes and lose more often. The exceptions do well and so they spread the myth that it is easy to make money trading in the stock markets on technical patterns and hearsay or gossip.

Some of these traders go beyond simple trading and venture into manipulation of stock prices. Their modus operandi is often to use multiple trading accounts and many brokers to create an illusion of active trading and interest in some stocks. In reality, they have control of the free float of these stocks and so are able to push their prices to unrealistic levels that do not reflect the underlying assets and profits of the companies.

Large numbers of unwary stock market traders usually get sucked into these counters, driven by greed and ignorance of fundamental analysis. When the music eventually stops, meaning the big players start to pull out of the stocks at their peak levels, these traders are left holding on to overpriced shares of poorly managed companies. Beware: do not fall into the traps that such manipulators have laid! If you apply the principles of valuation in Chapter 8, you should be able to determine whether a stock has become ridiculously (and sometimes, suspiciously) overvalued.

Manipulators know that there are many market participants who have the 'casino mentality' towards stocks, people who are excitedly looking for a fast buck. And indeed, the manipulators will pull a fast one on them.

It is very common in Singapore to hear people use the expression "play shares". It sounds fun and exciting, but reveals a very insidious attitude towards the stock market: that shares are something to be toyed with, frivolously, like punting at the casino, rather than carefully studied, analysed and approached in a measured manner. Please do not say "play shares". Say "invest in shares".

SGX witnessed the infamous bursting of the multibillion-dollar bubbles featuring Blumont Group, Asiasons Capital (now known as Attilan Group) and LionGold Corp in 2013. Their share prices had risen in a couple of years to phenomenal levels, despite their chequered profit record and uncertain business outlooks. When SGX eventually tightened its regulatory grip on the companies, their stocks went into free fall. From multibillion-dollar valuations, they have all fallen to small market capitalisations and prices per share are now (June 2018) 0.1 to 0.2 cent!

There has been, since then, a concerted effort to nail the culprits responsible for the fiasco. This episode resulted in a depressed market for at least three years, with low trading volumes and many companies delisting from SGX. Few companies have sought listing on SGX, preferring to list in Hong Kong or to remain private.

SGX and MAS have once again relooked the regulations, listing rules and corporate governance code. Changes have been made with the objective of ensuring more transparency by listed companies and orderly trading in the market. But over-regulation can lead to moribund markets where entrepreneurs are stifled by high costs and lengthy compliance lists in doing business or deals. Investors will also drift away from such markets. A balance is needed.

As we move towards lighter regulations with more emphasis on corporate governance, caveat emptor (buyer beware) comes into play. Investors have to bear the negative consequences of excessive risk-taking and being carried away by greed.

This self-discipline also applies to property investment. Do keep in mind that property is a good servant but a bad master.

It is OK to buy property in an upcycle, but when prices peak and a downturn takes over, you must be able to hold the illiquid assets and reduce your loans with the banks, using your cash reserves. If not, you could lose not only your property, but your own capital as well. Please see Chapter 6 for more on property and REITS.

The title to this chapter asks whether SGX stands for Singapore Gambling Exchange? The answer is that SGX (or any healthy stock exchange) is a place where you can actually build up your assets and eventually achieve financial independence, even if you are just an employee in a company or government body.

But it is the *attitude* you adopt towards the stock market and SGX that makes all the difference. I touched on this theme in Chapter 1 and will elaborate in other parts of the book. Read on!

CHAPTER 3

BANKS ARE NOT YOUR FRIENDS

The heading of this chapter sounds vitriolic. A sweeping statement. How can one even make such a statement and get away with it, I can hear bank apologists asking. There are many banks in the world and they have differing operating guidelines. Some are principled and have high social objectives in mind while pursuing their business objectives, I hear the banks and their supporters saying. Not all banks are out to exploit the consumer or businessman.

I do not disagree with these sentiments expressed by banking sector leaders and their investor or public relations officers. There are some good banks around but they are in the minority. It is the exceptions that make the rule, in other words.

So why have banks become this way, you might ask. Were they always like this or have they changed along the way and now have different priorities and objectives?

BANKS ARE PRIVATELY RUN AND PROFIT-MOTIVATED

It is a complex subject, and the reasons why banks are now the way they are – purely profit-motivated – are many and varied. But I think at the heart of the issue is the fact that most banks are now privately run, with many listed on various exchanges. This was not always so. The process of privatisation and then listing of banks on stock exchanges has really taken hold only in the last fifty years or so.

Why they were corporatised and privatised has been discussed and documented. Some banks put the social purpose high on their agenda and were not churning out any meaningful profits. In some cases, they needed additional funding to strengthen their capital bases, and their owners, usually the governments, were not willing or able to support them.

In other cases, the governments of the countries wanted to sell off state-owned assets like banks and so these were privatised and floated on stock exchanges. The governments involved were able to raise funds from such privatisations and use the money for other priorities, like healthcare, education, infrastructure or defence.

When banks were privatised and floated on stock exchanges, their managements had to focus more acutely on profitability. Besides employees and depositors, there was a new group of stakeholders – in the form of investors in the bank. As public entities, the banks' performance was available for scrutiny and investors could switch their loyalty among different banks quite easily.

So bank managements had to ensure they were bringing in profits commensurate with the capital invested. The good banks worked on expanding their franchises, in a range of activities as well as geographies. At the same time, they focused on reducing costs and improving operating margins.

All this was well and fine on the face of it. Banks grew steadily as economies expanded and they offered more services to consumers and businesses over wider geographies. Good bankers continued to be in demand, with their remuneration rising. But the pressure to grow and do better in profits and profitability meant something had to give.

Banks had to ensure their net average interest margins were healthy and growing. So, much effort was put into minimising interest payments to depositors and maximising what borrowers pay.

The different interest rates paid to the different kinds of deposit accounts were varied accordingly. Likewise, borrowers with their varied needs and profiles were charged different rates.

Of course, banks have other sources of funds, besides individual and corporate depositors. They can source for funds from the interbank market if rates are attractive and then lend out the monies to their customers in matching maturities or time periods. They could make decent interest or gross profit margins from such activity.

Today's universal banks are also active in a range of other activities, including stock and bond broking, investment banking and project financing. They collect vast amounts of fees on such activities and augment these with profits made on foreign exchange and money market operations.

In most of these activities, the banks are advantaged. They are in the front line, with their teams of skilled traders who have quick access to market intelligence, including research reports. The house traders in the brokerages have good insight into market activity and are better able to churn out profits for the bank on a daily basis. Similarly, the foreign exchange market is a global playground with banks in the forefront of intelligence and insights.

Individuals and companies, as clients of the banks, get some research and guidance from bank dealers. But they are inherently disadvantaged with higher brokerage rates and slower or limited access to market information and trends. No surprise then that individuals and corporates do less well than banks in these fields. There are no absolute numbers, but that is the strong sense I have of outcomes.

INTEREST RATES ON DEPOSITS

For risk-averse investors who prefer to simply keep their money in the banks, they may not lose anything over any period of time in nominal (dollar) terms. But they normally lose in real terms, that is, in the purchasing power of their savings as inflation outstrips the meagre interest earned. In Singapore, for instance, interest rates on deposits have been in a long-term decline. For the last few years, they have hit rock bottom, so that depositors are not able to even earn 1 percent on fixed deposits (FDs) of a year or longer.

If you are not willing to tie up your cash for a year at a time, then you will be paid 0.05-0.75 percent on your savings account.[1]

There are some foreign banks that periodically offer higher rates, but the rule among local banks DBS, OCBC and UOB is sub-one percent rates for FDs of all maturities, although there is the occasional promotion offering slightly above 1 per cent. Whatever the case, you will see your money in savings accounts and FDs erode in purchasing power as the average rate of inflation for the last three decades or so in Singapore is 1.7 percent, as mentioned in Chapter 1. There has been no

Chart 3.1 Interest rates have been in overall decline for many years

Source: The Monetary Authority of Singapore

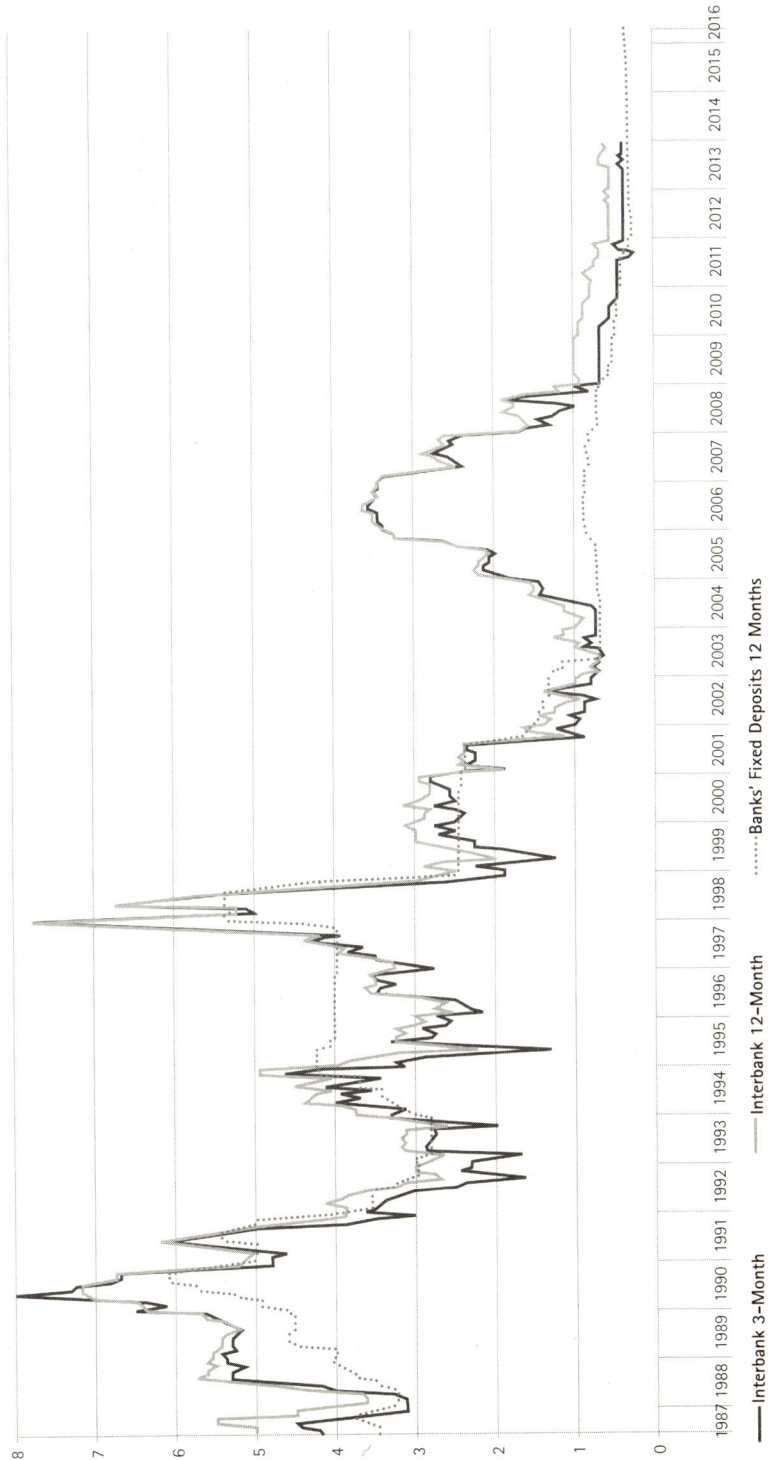

Interbank 3–Month
Interbank 12–Month
Banks' Fixed Deposits 12 Months

respite. POSB, the former Post Office Savings Bank, has also gradually cut its rates over the years to bring them in line with DBS, its parent.

In the 1960s and 1970s, POSB was under the purview of the Ministry of Finance and it seemed to put social objectives at the top of its agenda. Its deposits mostly ended up with the government or statutory boards, in the form of bonds purchased from them. POSB kept a small margin to cover its costs and passed the other earnings to its vast base of depositors. But all that changed when DBS took over POSB in November 1998 for a mere $1.6 b.

As a commercial bank, DBS had to look at how to best utilise the large deposit base built up by POSB since its inception in the 1960s. The depositors had come from all walks of life in Singapore and many had relied on the quasi-bank to earn a decent return on their savings. DBS though had a different objective. It had to try and maximise returns on the deposit base of the savings bank to appease its army of shareholders.

That meant a gradual shift away from the modus operandi of POSB. More of its deposits were put to work in the commercial lending sector where rates were higher. At the same time, it moved to adjust interest rates paid by POSB on deposits to bring them in line with its own rates which were lower across the board.

Today, POSB operates in the same way as DBS with its deposits deployed mostly for loans to consumers and corporations. Its current slogan is "Neighbours first, bankers second" and it continues to operate branches across the island. But other than external appearances and a few segmented niche products, there is very little difference between DBS and POSB in their approach to banking.

Profit is the key objective for POSB and DBS, just as it is for UOB and OCBC. DBS started as the Development Bank of Singapore in the 1960s. Its priority was to help in the development of the economy, through judicious loans to promising companies and individuals engaged in productive activity. Over the years, it has broadened its scope to become a universal bank involved in investment banking, foreign exchange, money market and stockbroking. DBS is growing and paying its employees and shareholders well.

But the same cannot be said for its depositors and borrowers. As mentioned earlier, the common man or woman, as a depositor, is not earning enough interest to even cover inflation.

Singaporeans are realising that banks are not giving them a fair return on their money, even though the deposits are risk-free. So they have been moving their money elsewhere, into bonds and foreign currency deposits. But the risks in these investments are higher. There has also been a huge move into property investment and Real Estate Investment Trusts or REITs. But here again, it is a different game and, commensurate with the rewards, the risks are higher (please see Chapter 6 for more on property and REITs).

On the borrowing side, companies and individuals have benefited from the lower rates prevailing for some time. But relative to the deposit rates, borrowing rates are significantly higher, with the banks keeping good margins. The lenders also keep their own interests as the top priority. So when a company or individual is in financial straits due to a business downturn or other factors, the banks usually do not hesitate to push for partial or full repayment of loans with interest accrued.

The bottom line is that commercial banks operate with a profit motive and with their own interests as top priority. They

"I'm afraid you will have to liquidate your property to pay the bank but the good news is, you now qualify for the Public Rental Scheme."

are no different from companies in most other industries. It is accepted that they have to manage their own risks and a large bank failure will be a setback for any economy. But the balance between serving society in a fair way and making a return on their business is not quite right.

Banks are putting their own interests too high up the priority list, so much so that you and I, the clients, cannot consider them our friends. They make all their money from us, the individuals and corporates, during good times. In bad times, they are quick to turn us away in favour of their own concerns. In some instances, they get into deep trouble themselves due to poor risk management and profligate lending. Then, they turn to the government for public money to survive!

DEREGULATION OF THE FINANCE INDUSTRY AND GLOBAL FINANCIAL CRISES

That is what happened during the Global Financial Crisis (GFC) of 2008/09 and the European Debt Crisis that began in late 2009. In the years leading up to these events, deregulation of the finance industry had been steadily taking place in the US. In 1999, Republican lawmaker Phil Gramm successfully led the effort that repealed most of the Glass-Steagall Act, which was a Depression-era law that kept Commercial Banking and Investment separated.

According to Forbes contributor Mike Collins: "only a year later Gramm inserted the new Commodity Futures Modernization Act into a must-pass budget bill that rocketed through the Congress. One part of this bill would prohibit the regulation of derivatives which allowed finance gurus to leverage and speculate with other people's money. By using derivatives, credit default swaps and other unregulated financial instruments, the big banks were able to chop up and resell loans and mortgages as repackaged securities or derivatives. The new securitization became globalized and eventually affected the world economy.

"After the creation of new financial tools (like credit default swaps and derivatives) as well as more access to everybody's money; the banks began to do *high risk gambling just like a big casino*. The new financial tools were backed by the government so that taxpayers would get hung with the bill."

The reckless risk-taking by many large banks – from the dizzy dispensation of mortgage loans to risky "subprime" borrowers, to taking on monumental debt to plunge into mortgage-backed securities (an investment instrument based on loans to property buyers) – set the stage for the catastrophic global financial crisis in 2008/09, when the 158-year-old investment bank Lehman Brothers collapsed and numerous other US financial institutions like Citigroup and Goldman Sachs needed to be bailed out by the government and/or various investors.

To highlight the pathological ebullience and impetuosity that bankers are capable of, Lehman Brothers had a gearing – the ratio of total debt to shareholder's equity – of 31 times in 2007. Yes, their debt was a mind-boggling *31 times* greater than their net assets. Somehow the MBAs, CFAs and quantitative finance experts working there thought it was sound risk management.

Collins adds, "The operating principles of the big banks is a cesspool of greed, ethics and criminal intent and they give a very bad name to free market capitalism. During the housing bubble Wall Street was considered the heart and soul of free market capitalism, but when they were in danger of total collapse they fell on their knees as socialists, begging the government and tax payers to bail them out."[2]

SINGAPORE BANKS

Well, thankfully the Singapore banks are very well-regulated, so there isn't much "criminal intent" amongst them. But it would still be naive to regard them as your friends.

They too tend to overly prioritise their own interest – pardon the pun – at the expense of society and the common man. In recent times, the three local banks DBS, UOB and OCBC have all reported excellent results. All three posted double-digit growth in the fourth quarter of 2017. For the whole of 2017, OCBC grew net profit by 19 percent to $4.2 b, UOB by 9 percent to $3.4 b, and DBS by 4 percent to $4.4 b. DBS, celebrating its fiftieth anniversary, was particularly generous with its dividends. It proposed a 60 cents per share final dividend plus a special dividend of 50 cents as a one-time return of capital buffers that had been built up and to mark the anniversary – on top of a 33-cent interim dividend that had been announced at the half-year mark. In 2016, only 60 cents was paid out for the whole year. Following the full-year results for 2017, the bank also announced that it would pay out $1.20 a year going forward.

The banks have done very well for themselves and their shareholders in an environment of rising interest rates as the US Federal Reserve tightens monetary policy. Lending rates are creeping up as bond yields rise. But the banks have been slow to pass on their gains to ordinary savers – deposit rates remain pitifully low.

Ever since DBS acquired POSB in 1998, the group has held such a dominant position in the local money market and bank network that it has a disproportionate pricing power in savings interest rates. The rather stingy rates they are paying (as low as 0.05 percent on the first $350,000 in a savings account[3]) is not helpful to the moms and pops in the heartlands who save their money with POSB.

When one asks the banks why deposit rates are so low, they tend to say that the market decides. However, this is not a satisfactory explanation for the delay in deposit rate hikes when monetary conditions are tightening and interest rates in general are on the uptrend.

Singapore banks are also not immune to the excessive greed and risk-taking that have engulfed some of their western peers. All three were caught by the sharp downturn in the oil and gas industry as they had lent extensively to companies in the offshore support services sector. One example is Swiber Holdings, which ran into deep financial trouble and has been under judicial management since October 2016. DBS and UOB both extended loans to them – and the former's exposure was $700 m comprising loans, bonds and off-balance sheet items[4]. I have never been impressed with Swiber's management and am quite astonished that DBS deemed fit to lend so much to them. And this is certainly not the only shaky company that the local banks have extended heavy financing to.

As mentioned earlier, banks are not the friends of either corporations or individuals. If you are a borrower, they lend gladly on a sunny day but take away your umbrella on a rainy day. And if you are a shareholder or even a depositor, their sometimes excessive or even reckless risk-taking can hurt you (in the latter case if the bank should fold up). *So, should I pull my money out of the bank and keep it in a Milo tin?*

No, that won't be necessary. I am not suggesting that we stop dealing with banks altogether.

It is still perfectly fine to deposit your money with a bank (preferably one that has a strong balance sheet and conservative financial management), as long as the sum of money you put in is covered by deposit insurance. In Singapore, for instance, in the event that a bank fails, all of a depositor's eligible accounts with that bank will be aggregated and insured up to $50,000[5]. Thus if you have $100,000 in cash savings, it would be sensible to split it equally between two banks. Your savings would then be fully insured if the worst should happen.

It is also fine to borrow from a bank, but the only two things I personally would borrow for are (a) to buy a home and (b) to start or grow a business. *Try to avoid or at least minimise borrowing for consumption spending,* for instance to go on a holiday or buy the latest iPhone. Such debt is invariably unsecured (no collateral), for instance credit card or credit line debt, and attracts very high rates of interest (around 26 percent per annum in Singapore[6]). It is very well-known in the world of finance that the credit card division is among the most profitable units at a bank – and the reason is obvious. Just think about it – banks pay you as little as 0.05 percent a year if you deposit with them, and charge you 26 percent if you borrow on your credit card.

An old saying goes, "A man in debt is caught in a net." Thus it is only sensible to avoid debt if we can. Of course we sometimes have no choice but to borrow to buy a home, and provided we choose a property that is within our means and also priced at a reasonable level, it can be a wise financial decision as every mortgage payment we make increases our family's assets and builds its financial foundation. A well-selected property in an area with development potential can also appreciate in value over time. Borrowing to start or grow a business can also be an intelligent use of debt as it gives us the opportunity to realise our entrepreneurial ambitions, be our own boss and possibly grow rich. As with investing, we must do our due diligence and work out a strong business plan.

Borrowing for consumption, however, is usually foolish unless it is for something we critically need. It goes against the sound financial principles this book advocates, primarily to save as much as we can to provide the capital for investment. Borrowing to fulfil our materialistic whims and desires is the exact opposite of this good financial sense – instead of strengthening our base, it will steadily chip away at our net worth. It can even lead to bankruptcy.

This is where, yet again, you have to be wary of banks. I am sure you have noticed the ubiquitous advertisements for credit cards and credit lines. A picture of a happy individual putting his feet up at a five-star beach resort, or holding her big shopping bags with a rapturous smile on her face, or cradling the guitar he has coveted for weeks. A message along the lines of living the life you've always dreamed of *right now*, giving yourself the life that *you deserve*, how *cool* and *stylish* you would be. This is all emotional manipulation to prey on your mental weaknesses – beware!

Be careful also not to be seduced by the endless 'promos' and 'discounts' on credit cards. It can tempt you to get too many credit cards and fall into the absurdity of "spend more to save more". You will also not be able to keep track of all the promotions and will turn into a slave to all these marketing campaigns. I would suggest that you maintain no more than two, maybe three, cards. Cancel all those that are not essential to your lifestyle – getting an extra 3 percent discount here and 5 percent rebate there is not worth the mental strain of being buried under plastic, junk mail and worst of all, debt at exorbitant interest rates.

SHOULD I GET THE BANK TO INVEST MY MONEY?

Walk into any bank branch today and if the staff notice that you have a sizeable balance in your savings account, they might try to sell you some kind of investment product.

My most considered advice is this: *Generally speaking, it is a bad idea to get the bank to invest your money unless you are a private banking client receiving close personal attention from a capable team of private bankers.* For mass-market customers (ordinary Joes and Janes), the bank usually tries to sell you some kind of investment 'product' or 'plan' that involves certain assets (e.g. stocks and bonds) packaged with specific terms and conditions. If the correlated assets perform well, the returns will be higher; if not, you will get less at the end of the day. Such products typically offer an average return that is a few percentage points higher than a fixed deposit. Your capital may be fully protected, partially protected or not protected at all.

I do not believe that such investment 'packages' are worth putting your money into because they are packaged in a way that is *more in the bank's favour than yours.* If you read the fine print, you will likely find that there are high fees involved, which will steadily whittle away your profits. In any case, chances are that the profits won't be very high even *before* the fees are deducted. Why? Because these products usually involve investments being made using *passive strategies.* If you are a mass-market customer without millions of dollars to invest, the bankers will not *actively* manage your capital as they do not find it worthwhile to devote such attention to you.

You would be better off doing the passive investment yourself – DIY! Just follow a sound passive investing strategy such as the ones described in Chapter 5 of this book. By putting your money into low-cost instruments such as exchange-traded funds or ETFs, you will avoid the high fees inherent in most bank investment products. In the long run – and with the astonishing power of compounding – even a couple of percentage points of lower cost per year makes a huge difference to your returns.

In extreme cases, some of these bank investment 'products' or 'plans' have inflicted 70–100 percent losses on their customers. The most notorious case could be the Lehman Brothers Minibond saga that began in 2008, when the famous Lehman Brothers investment bank filed for bankruptcy. The so-called 'minibonds' (which weren't really bonds at all, but credit-linked notes assembled using complex derivatives) and related products such as High Notes 5 and Jubilee Series3 LinkEarner Notes were sold by a number of banks in Singapore. These products became worthless or next to worthless as their value was linked to Lehman Brothers' financial situation. In Singapore, bank customers had pumped in some $500 m into such 'structured investment products' and in Hong Kong, the sum was HK$20 b.

After public protests in both cities, banks that had distributed these toxic 'products' began a settlement process with their disgruntled customers. Ultimately, some received as much as 96.5 percent of their capital back, while others got one-third or less. Banks in both cities were taken to task for mis-selling, representing these products as safe investments (a bit of a stretch, considering that Lehman Brothers, as mentioned earlier, had 31 times more debt than net assets). The victims were often the elderly, less educated and vulnerable.[7, 8, 9]

So, for most of us, it is usually unwise to let banks invest your money. But why do I make an exception for some *private banking clients*? If you are a high net-worth individual (especially a *very* high net-worth individual with over US$5 m in assets, excluding your primary residence), you will be able to get a team of bankers to pay close personal attention to your investments and carry out active strategies for you. *If these bankers are capable investors and asset managers*, they may be able to generate outstanding returns for you that will justify the substantial fees they charge.

But I must insert some crucial caveats here. Make sure that your team of bankers is indeed a highly competent one before you place a significant chunk of your assets in their care. You can give them a smaller amount to manage for a year or two first to let them prove their level of skill and professionalism. *Make sure that they are ethical and act with your best interests at heart.* You can also assess them in this area over time before you commit a larger sum. Finally, *you must always take ownership of your investments even if your money is being managed by the most gifted bankers on earth*. There is no running away from doing your homework: you need to develop at least a sound basic understanding of what they are doing with your money. It's your money!

Be conscious also that bankers come and go. One or more of the outstanding, upstanding team members in charge of your account may suddenly leave for another bank – in which case the level of talent and integrity can change drastically. You need to monitor their performance and character on an ongoing basis.

The countless lawsuits filed by wealthy people against banks are valuable lessons. When we read the details of such lawsuits, we find that sometimes even billionaires fall asleep while delegating the work of investment to their bankers, or following their advice.

You may want to outsource some of the hard work; but you don't want to outsource away your entire financial future, and your family's security.

Whether you are an ultra-high net-worth individual with US$30 m in liquid assets or a regular Joe with a few thousand dollars, let Common Sense prevail, first and foremost. *Know what you are doing.* And make people earn your trust before you give it to them.

---

1   According to the websites of all three local banks DBS, OCBC and UOB, the basic savings deposit rate was 0.05 percent as of 25 Jan 2018. They provided slightly higher rates under various terms and conditions, such as crediting your monthly salary or depositing a fixed amount every month, or not withdrawing from the account in a given month. These augmented rates ranged from 0.35 to 0.75 percent – still well below the average rate of inflation in Singapore.

2   "The Big Bank Bailout", Mike Collins, Forbes, 14 Jul 2015 https://www.forbes.com/sites/mikecollins/2015/07/14/the-big-bank-bailout/#396644c52d83

3   According to the DBS website on 15 Feb 2018 https://www.dbs.com.sg/personal/rates-online/deposit-rates.page

4   "DBS has S$700 m exposure to Swiber", Jamie Lee, Tan Hwee Hwee and
    Anita Gabriel, *Business Times*, 29 Jul 2016 http://www.businesstimes.com.
    sg/companies-markets/dbs-has-s700m-exposure-to-swiber

5   Singapore Deposit Insurance Corporation website, 27 Jan 2018 https://
    www.sdic.org.sg

6   For perspective, remember that the same bank is paying you as little as
    0.05 percent on your savings account.

7   "Lehman Brothers Minibond Saga", Singapore Infopedia, National
    Library Board Singapore, http://eresources.nlb.gov.sg/infopedia/articles/
    SIP_1654_2010-03-19.html

8   "Five years later, what has the minibond scandal taught us?", Tom Holland,
    South China Morning Post, 18 Sep 2013 http://www.scmp.com/business/
    article/1311841/five-years-later-what-has-mini-bond-scandal-taught-us

9   "The good inside the bad", *The Economist*, 31 Mar 2011 http://www.
    economist.com/node/18486397

CHAPTER 4

ROUTES TO FINANCIAL INDEPENDENCE

GETTING THERE WHICHEVER LANE YOU TRAVEL IN

All of us have the desire to retire comfortably when the time comes. It is a common aspiration to live our 'golden' years in relative comfort, maintaining our lifestyle as it was during our economically active years. If possible, we would want our dependants to also be able to live with us without too many financial worries.

But of course, not all of us are blessed with a large income that allows us to build up our savings and investment portfolio rapidly. Fret not, however. For those of us who are of immigrant stock, just think of how some of our forefathers – for instance Chinese and Indian immigrants who arrived in Singapore and Malaysia (then Malaya) with little more than the clothes on their backs in the 1930s – scraped and saved even while earning a pittance as coolies and menial workers, to eventually become land and business owners.

If even they with their miserable wages could still save, then surely so can we today, even if our wages are on the low end of the scale. Of course I am not saying that it is easy. It takes all your reserves of willpower, but if there is a will, there is a way. One great challenge we face today, compared to our ancestors, is the pervasive ideology of consumerism. All around us are advertisements and 'promotion' campaigns for everything from smartphones to perfumes to holidays. Malls have become more and more seductive, with an ever-expanding array of temptations in a globalised world. Big corporations hire top neuroscientists to help design their marketing campaigns to powerfully persuade – even brainwash – us to buy their products. At the same time credit cards are mushrooming, and their promoters and advertisers seek to instil in us a "spend today, worry tomorrow" mentality.

Gambling too has become more and more prevalent, with casinos springing up in the physical world as well as online. Scams are also spreading like wildfire, with the crafty and devious capitalising on the reach of the Internet and social media to relieve millions of their money (see Chapter 9 on scams).

In other words, financial traps and pitfalls are everywhere.

But if you educate yourself about all these, and are clear in your goals and firm in your resolve, *you can protect yourself and take steps towards financial freedom whether you are a high, middle or low income earner* – as long as your income is slightly more than enough to cover the barest necessities. And this is the key message of this chapter – that *there are several routes to financial independence.* Whether you are travelling in the fast lane (high earner), middle lane (medium earner) or slow lane (low earner), the road still leads to a good place (financial independence) for those who have the willingness to learn how to drive sensibly and navigate the obstacles and hazards – plus the fortitude to go the distance. You also need the resilience to bounce back from setbacks and mistakes.

I will present to you case studies of the drive to financial freedom for the three different income groups. The first one (high income) uses myself as the case study as I was blessed to be promoted to senior positions during my career. The second (middle income) and third (low income) are hypothetical case studies using figures that are as realistic and accurate as I can find.

GENERAL PRINCIPLES

There is no shortage of advice in the marketplace as to how we should prepare for retirement. Insurance companies would rather you buy their policies and rely on them to provide for your old age. In Singapore, there is the Central Provident Fund (CPF) which requires citizens to keep aside a portion of their earned income each month, to be accumulated until they are at least fifty-five years of age. After fifty-five, some withdrawals are allowed with the remainder kept aside to pay for medical costs as well as to provide a modest monthly income beyond the retirement age.

Some people prefer to invest their savings in properties, in addition to their own home.

These instruments or options are all useful and can help you in planning for retirement. Through them, as well as stocks and bonds, you can build up a nest egg of assets and recurrent, passive income.

So sit down and think about how you want to prepare for your family's future and how you can, on a sustained basis, balance your expenses and savings with your income. You must have the will to keep aside a sum of money, a percentage of your earned income, for the future. Tied to that is the need to project your income and budget your expenses, so the savings can be realised. Once you have a clear picture of what you can save each month and year, you will be motivated to achieve the sums.

Case Study One: The Fast Lane – High-Income Earners

I was fortunate to belong to this group of wage earners, so I will share my own personal experiences, without going into the exact numbers (to protect my family's privacy). After that, I will provide a more specific case study of a hypothetical high-income family, using more specific and detailed numbers.

Your expenses budget is personal to you. In my case, I divide the annual budget into broad categories covering household expenses (this is the biggest item, comprising food, utility and telephone bills; children's allowances and various other items); my own and my spouse's spending money; education for the children; support for my handicapped brother; running costs of two cars; insurance premiums; income and property tax; holiday and travel; and last but not least, donations to worthwhile causes.

My wife, Nisha, takes care of the household bills through a monthly transfer to her which includes an allowance. She is a full-time homemaker who works for the community on a voluntary basis. I also provide a certain amount each year for unforeseen family-related expenses. This is for a medical emergency, house repairs and replacement of items, or other unexpected cash out-go. Further, I have been setting aside a fixed amount every month for Nisha and the children for many years; this is their endowment account for their personal use in future. So, for my family, the expenses budget covering all the items described above totals about $200,000 per annum or $16,667 a month. I would not say we live an ostentatious lifestyle. The children, now all grown up, are also practical in their spending habits.

In addition, my budget provides for some investment in the future. The insurance premiums cover the family for medical crises as well as life. The life policies are profit-sharing, meaning they have accumulated bonuses over the years and feature surrender cash values. Nisha has also built up significant savings in the household expenses account, thanks to her prudent spending.

The children are encouraged to save part of their allowances and this habit has put them in good stead now as working adults. As at this year, 2018, two of them are in the workforce and gradually building up their savings. Our family has been fortunate to be able to put aside a significant portion of my annual income for the future. The percentage has varied, from a low level when I was just starting out as a reporter in the *Business Times* to a much higher level when I was Managing Director in DBS (1996–2000) and then, later, as CEO and editor-in-chief of MediaCorp Press which published the *TODAY* newspaper (2003–2006).

But *as my work income rose, I did not automatically adopt a more expensive lifestyle.* This is a crucial point. Many people fall into the financial trap of always upgrading their lifestyle in step with their income – which is why many high earners, with tragic irony, can never break out of being a wage slave. My family's lifestyle is based mainly on our needs, and not driven by wants. I would say that of all the values held by our immigrant forefathers in Singapore, thrift is both one of the most precious and the most eroded in succeeding generations.

Our home, a semi-detached house in Singapore, is simply furnished to harmonise with nature. Browns and greens dominate and wastage of any kind is discouraged. We have two cars, both Toyotas, and they are shared by all members of the family, with public transport also frequently used.

Every individual and family will have to work out their own numbers based on their personal income levels and living style. In working on a financial plan, the family has to aim not just for savings to be used in the sunset years of the older members. If possible, *each couple should aim for financial independence. By that, I mean you invest and build up your passive income to a point where it covers your expenses on a regular basis* and there is no need to dig into the principal amounts or investments. It would be better still if the entire family can sustain itself permanently through its savings and investment strategies. This is not an easy achievement, but it can be done through hard work in building careers, discipline and prudent management of earnings. Work out your long-term financial plan and once you are on the way to implementing it, remember to first set aside cash equivalent to six months of family expenses. This will be separate from your investment account and will tide you over in bad periods.

As for insurance policies, my approach has been to go for term policies where the premiums are low and the coverage high. For a young, growing family, that is what is really needed: a cover for unforeseen situations. Group term policies, such as those through the Automobile Association of Singapore and SAFRA, offer good value. *I prefer not to mix insurance with investment, so investment-linked policies are not my choice.* When you conflate insurance and investment, it is easy to get confused as the two activities are fundamentally different. You also hand over too much control of your investments to outside parties – in this case the insurance companies or fund management companies that they outsource the investing work to.

But each of my family members has a long-term life policy, besides the term policies. We felt that it would be good to have some whole life coverage, besides the term coverage which ends by a specified age. Do read the fine print of each policy document to understand its terms and conditions before you commit to it. For some policies, the premiums are adjusted with age and so they become prohibitive when you need them most in your later years!

For Singaporeans, savings in the CPF form an important component of their retirement savings, but that may not be sufficient on their own. This is because most Singaporeans use the bulk of their CPF savings to buy homes. However, private and public property values have appreciated over the years, so people have nice nest eggs to fall back on. Those who are asset-rich and cash-poor can extract cash from their homes in various ways, including renting out rooms or downgrading to smaller flats.

Cash in the CPF account actually earns more than what banks are prepared to pay on deposits. Older citizens are generally paid more on their balances, with the rate going as high as 5 percent on core savings in Retirement Accounts. So one should not be in a hurry to withdraw savings in CPF if there is no dire need for cash. Let the money grow in the CPF retirement account until it is really needed.

After providing for all budgeted expenses, emergency family cash and insurance premiums, you should invest your savings for better returns. Fixed deposits bear no risk, but the returns on them are paltry. So consider other investments related to property, stocks, bonds and collectibles. Bear in mind that investments are for the long term and so they should be separated from the family expenses account.

For me, the preference has been for stocks and shares rather than property, bonds or collectibles. I started as a reporter with the Companies Desk of *Business Times* in 1977. As I interviewed many companies, I got to know them better. I learnt to read balance sheets and profit/loss statements and to understand business models of various listed entities. Almost naturally, I started investing in listed Singapore and Malaysian companies.

My aim even at that time, when I was just twenty-seven years old, was to go for value investing and to grow my investment income over the years. The ultimate aim was financial independence by the ripe-old-age of fifty-five years. I calculated that if I were to get married and grow a family, the expenses could rise to, say, $120,000 per annum. If I could earn 4 percent in dividend or interest income on a portfolio built up to $3 m, the family expenses would be fully covered with the principal untouched. So I set to work putting aside savings, and investing in promising, well-managed companies. It has been a long slog through many ups and downs.

But I am happy to say the goal has been more than achieved. Over the years, I have pulled out my original capital and the portfolio is now made up entirely of profits from 1977. Since 2000 or so, dividends from the portfolio have not been reinvested. Instead they have largely been channelled to cover family expenses, at least in part. This approach was aimed at reducing dependence on job income and eventually achieving total financial independence, i.e. no dependence at all on job income cashflow.

So when did my family achieve financial independence? This happened in 2005 when I, the main family breadwinner, turned fifty-five. Interest and dividend income became sufficient to cover family expenses, which were about $200,000 per annum. The expenses included income tax payable, insurance premiums and cash transferred to the endowment accounts of dependant family members.

The reality is that job income dwindles as we get older. To maintain a decent lifestyle, it is essential to build savings and invest them prudently while in your prime earning years. It is hard work, but it has to be done. All families should aim for this ideal: total financial independence through good financial planning.

Now, I shall provide a breakdown of the income and expenses of a hypothetical high-income family *(not mine)* to show how it can achieve financial freedom. *It must be stressed that high income does not automatically mean it is easy to become financially liberated.* Many people have high earnings and even higher expenses, and end up in financial bondage or even disaster (the late Michael Jackson is a good example).

Monthly income = $18,972[1]
After tax income = $18,401[2]

Breakdown of monthly expenses

Mortgage payments for 1,249 sq ft condo unit at Dover Parkview, 11th to 15th floor[3,] based on 20-year loan: $6,452

Condo maintenance/ facilities fees: $340

Utilities: $180 (moderate use of air-conditioning)

Food and beverage: $1,938 ($18 per person per day, multiplied by average household size of 3.53 persons and 30.5 days a month. This assumes a mean cost of $6 per meal, which should accommodate a comfortable but not extravagant lifestyle. Most meals at home, food courts or coffee shops, with the occasional restaurant meal.)

Transport (inclusive of car loan payments for one mid-sized Japanese car[4], fuel, car insurance and some use of public transportation): $1,300

Internet/ cable TV/ mobile phone subscriptions: $240

Allowances to parents (of both spouses): $1,000

Children's school/ daycare and private tuition expenses (a norm in Singapore): $2,400 (for 2 children)

Insurance: $1,000

Domestic helper (including salary, levies and other expenses): $1,000

Yearly holiday: $600 (assuming an intermediate destination like Japan in most years and a far-flung destination like Europe every five years. Estimated average annual cost $7,200 divided by 12 months.)

Entertainment: $300

Miscellaneous expenses including household repairs: $300

Total monthly expenses: $17,050

Therefore for the family in this case study,
Monthly savings = $18,401 − $17,050
            = $1,351

Annual savings = $16,212 for the first 20 years (while paying mortgage) and $93,636 from the 21st year (mortgage fully paid up)

This family will take 6.3 years to build an emergency fund of six months' expenses (17,050 x 6)/16,212 = 6.3 years. Thereafter, if we assume that they continuously invest their $16,212 annual savings ($93,636 from the 21st year) and achieve a 6 percent compounded return[5], how long will it take for them to achieve financial freedom?

Table 4.1: Long-term returns for high-income family (S$)

Year	Annual Investment	Net Return	Total	Remarks
1	0	0	0	Building emergency fund
2	0	0	0	Building emergency fund
3	0	0	0	Building emergency fund
4	0	0	0	Building emergency fund
5	0	0	0	Building emergency fund
6	0	0	0	Building emergency fund
7	11,348.00	680.88	12,028.88	Approximately first 4 months building emergency fund
8	16,212.00	1,694.45	29,935.33	
9	16,212.00	2,768.84	48,916.17	
10	16,212.00	3,907.69	69,035.86	
11	16,212.00	5,114.87	90,382.73	
12	16,212.00	6,394.48	112,969.22	
13	16,212.00	7,750.87	136,932.09	
14	16,212.00	9,188.65	162,332.74	
15	16,212.00	10,712.68	189,257.42	
16	16,212.00	12,328.17	217,797.59	
17	16,212.00	14,040.58	248,050.16	
18	16,212.00	15,855.73	280,117.89	
19	16,212.00	17,779.79	314,109.69	
20	16,212.00	19,819.30	350,140.99	
21	93,636.00	26,626.62	470,403.61	Mortgage fully paid – can increase savings and investment
22	93,636.00	33,842.38	597,881.98	
23	93,636.00	41,914.08	733,009.98	
24	93,636.00	49,598.70	876,243.77	
25	93,636.00	58,192.79	1,028,072.55	
26	93,636.00	67,302.51	1,189,011.06	
27	93,636.00	76,958.82	1,359,605.89	
28	93,636.00	87,194.51	1,540,436.40	
29	93,636.00	98,044.34	1,732,116.75	
30	93,636.00	109,545.16	1,935,297.91	
31	93,636.00	121,736.03	2,150,669.94	
32	93,636.00	134,658.36	2,378,964.30	
33	93,636.00	148,356.02	2,620,956.32	

Table 4.1 shows that a high-income family in Singapore can amass an investment portfolio worth *$1,935,297.91* after thirty years (the first 6.3 years are for building up an emergency fund, during which no investment can take place). This *excludes* the value of their home, which should be fully paid up by then, as well as a $102,300 emergency fund to cushion against unforeseen events.

Is the above investment portfolio enough to retire on? If their portfolio contains a good proportion of stocks and/or real estate investment trusts (REITs) with a decent dividend yield[6] (or bonds with a decent yield), it should not be too difficult to achieve a 5 percent overall portfolio yield, which would produce an annual passive income of *$96,765.* In *today's dollars*, assuming the average inflation rate of 1.7 percent persists into the future, that would be *$58,357 a year* or *$4,863 a month.*

To the average couple, that should be a very comfortable retirement income. But the problem that arises here is that this household's current expenses are $10,598 a month (excluding the mortgage, which they would have fully serviced within twenty years) in today's dollars. If we exclude the children's education expenses, which should no longer apply after thirty years, and also food and beverage, utility and transport expenses for their children (who should be self-supporting by then), their monthly expenditure would be about *$6,928 – still $2,065 above their future retirement income measured in today's dollars. Another way of looking at it is that their retirement income will be about 70 percent of what it will cost to maintain their current lifestyle.*

So, will this couple of breadwinners be able to retire comfortably and happily after thirty years of following this financial regimen? I would say yes, provided they are prepared to make moderate adjustments to their lifestyle. For instance, they could reduce the number of long-haul holiday trips or replace some trips to Japan or Korea with visits to Thailand or Vietnam.

If this couple wish to have a more cushy retirement, they could consider delaying retirement for a further three years (a total of thirty-three years of working, saving and investment) if their health permits. They would then have a *$2,620,956.32* nest egg. A 5 percent dividend yield on that would amount to $131,048 a year in dividends, equivalent to $75,134 in today's dollars ($6,261 a month). They would be able to enjoy an almost identical standard of living as when they were working!

You might have noticed that this hypothetical family has not done as well as mine has. One reason is that I ascribed a modest 6 percent compound rate of return to their investments, whereas I achieved approximately 15.5 percent on my own portfolio (see Chapter 7, Buy Growth Stocks in Crisis (GSIC), for details). If the family develops a higher level of skill in investing and become good active investors, they can do much better than the conservative estimates in Table 4.1.

Moreover, I crafted the case study based on the kind of lifestyle that I believe the typical Singaporean family with this income level would be willing to accept – moderately frugal, but with a good dose of frills. If they were willing to accept, for instance, budget holidays every other year or to live in a smaller, say 900-sq ft, apartment, they would be able to build their emergency fund more quickly and start investing much earlier, allowing their profits to compound over more years and accumulate much more rapidly at a higher savings rate.

If they chose a 900-sq ft apartment and their mortgage was 25 percent lower at $4,839 a month, they would more than double their rate of savings to $2,964 a month (from $1,351). Their emergency fund ($92,622) would be achieved in only 2.6 years rather than 6.3. And their investment portfolio would be worth a whopping *$3,213,145.22* after thirty years (as opposed to $1,935,297.91) – and $4,142,892.91 after thirty-three years.

A key lesson in the case study has been this: even a high-income family needs to be frugal to achieve financial freedom. If they were, for example, to buy a new BMW, eat at expensive restaurants every day or travel to the US every year for a vacation, they would find that even if they earn $18,972 a month, they could be trapped in financial bondage their entire lives. Food for thought!

Case Study Two: The Middle Lane – Middle-Income Earners

The median monthly household income from work in Singapore was $8,846 in 2016.[7]

The average resident employed household size in the same year was 3.53 persons.[8]

After income tax, the median household would have a disposable income of *$8,754 a month*. Income tax is $92 a month ($1,100 a year), assuming that the household income of $8,846 is earned by the couple in equal proportion, meaning that each one brings in $4,423 a month or $53,076 a year. Based on Singapore income tax rates, which are low by international standards, each of the two breadwinners would pay about $550 after factoring in tax reliefs such as those for children, national service and mandatory contributions to Central Provident Fund.

Using these figures, we can work out the expenses and potential savings of a household that is *thrifty* and *determined to achieve financial liberation.* Of course, they can still enjoy life and have the occasional luxury, but there needs to be significant short-term sacrifices for long-term security and comfort.

Breakdown of monthly expenses (based in part on the lifestyle of a friend who achieved financial independence at age forty-two through disciplined thrift)
Mortgage payments for a three-bedroom, 108-sq m HDB (public housing), 7th to 9th storey apartment in Yishun Central (5 minutes' walk to MRT station) on a 20-year loan[9]: $1,612

Utilities: $150 (this can be lower without use of air-conditioning – invest in good quality fans! The figure also takes into account regular government subsidies for HDB residents, which offset this expense.)

Food and beverage: $1,292 ($12 per person per day, multiplied by 3.53 persons and 30.5 days a month. This assumes a mean cost of $4 per meal, which is achievable if you have breakfast at home, frequently choose the hawker centre/coffee shop over the food court/restaurant, and bring your own water instead of buying a drink. It's healthier, too! Oh – and keep your distance from Starbucks!)

Transport: $300 (a very important aspect of thrift in Singapore is to do without a car, as cars here are among the most expensive in the world due to hefty taxes. Thus this number is based on daily bus and MRT travel, which is relatively affordable – and schoolchildren/ senior citizens enjoy concessionary fares. It also makes allowance for the occasional taxi ride.)

Internet/ cable TV/ mobile phone subscriptions: $180

Allowances to parents (of both spouses): $1,000

Children's school/ daycare and private tuition expenses (a norm in Singapore): $1,200 (for 2 children)

Insurance: $800

Yearly holiday: $500 (assuming an intermediate destination like Japan. Estimated total cost $6,000 divided by 12 months.)

Entertainment: $100

Miscellaneous expenses including household repairs: $200

Total monthly expenses: $7,334

Two very important lifestyle choices here are doing without a car and a domestic helper. These two combined would add at least $2,500 to monthly expenses if one were to opt for them. As mentioned earlier, I believe firmly that a middle-income family in Singapore should really try to do without a car if they desire to achieve financial freedom at a relatively early age, due to the astronomical cost of a car here. If the family chooses to hire a domestic helper, it can counterbalance this by buying an apartment that is new and subsidised, smaller and/or in a less expensive location.

For the family in this case study,

Monthly savings = $8,754 - $7,334 = $1,420

Annual savings = $17,040 for the first twenty years (while paying mortgage) and $36,384 from the 21st year (mortgage fully paid up)

This family will take about three years to build an emergency fund of six months' expenses (44,004/17,040 = 2.6 years). Thereafter, if we assume that they continuously invest their $17,040 annual savings and achieve a 6 percent annual compounded return, how long will it take for them to achieve financial freedom?

Table 4.2: Long-term returns for middle-income family (S$)[10]

Year	Annual Investment	Net Return	Total	Remarks
1	0	0	0	Building emergency fund
2	0	0	0	Building emergency fund
3	0	0	0	Building emergency fund
4	17,040.00	1,022.40	18,062.40	
5	17,040.00	2,106.14	37,208.54	
6	17,040.00	3,254.91	57,503.46	
7	17,040.00	4,472.61	79,016.06	
8	17,040.00	5,763.36	101,819.43	
9	17,040.00	7,131.57	125,990.99	
10	17,040.00	8,581.86	151,612.85	
11	17,040.00	10,119.17	178,772.02	
12	17,040.00	11,748.72	207,560.75	
13	17,040.00	13,476.04	238,076.79	
14	17,040.00	15,307.01	270,423.80	
15	17,040.00	17,247.83	304,711.63	
16	17,040.00	19,305.10	341,056.72	
17	17,040.00	21,485.80	379,582.53	
18	17,040.00	23,797.35	420,419.88	
19	17,040.00	26,247.59	463,707.47	

20	17,040.00	28,844.85	509,592.32	
21	36,384.00	32,758.58	578,734.90	Mortgage fully paid – can increase savings and investment
22	36,384.00	36,907.13	652,026.03	
23	36,384.00	41,304.60	729,714.63	
24	36,384.00	45,965.92	812,064.55	
25	36,384.00	50,906.91	899,355.47	
26	36,384.00	56,144.37	991,883.83	
27	36,384.00	61,696.07	1,089,963.90	
28	36,384.00	67,580.87	1,193,928.78	
29	36,384.00	73,818.77	1,304.131.54	
30	36,384.00	80,430.93	1,420,946.48	
31	36,384.00	87,439.83	1,544,770.31	
32	36,384.00	94,869.26	1,676,023.56	
33	36,384.00	102,744.45	1,815,152.02	

Let's crunch the numbers and see.

Table 4.2 shows that the median family in Singapore can amass an investment portfolio worth *$1,420,946.48* after thirty years (to be conservative, we shall assume that the first three years – rather than the 2.6 years we earlier estimated – are for building up an emergency fund, during which no investment can take place). And this *excludes* the value of their home, which should be fully paid up by then, as well as a $44,004 emergency fund to cushion against unforeseen events.

Is the above investment portfolio enough to retire on? If their portfolio contains a good proportion of stocks and/or Real Estate Investment Trusts (REITs) with a decent dividend yield (or bonds with a decent yield), it should not be too difficult to achieve a 5 percent overall portfolio yield, which would produce an annual passive income of *$71,047*. In *today's dollars*, assuming the average inflation rate of 1.7 percent persists into the future, that would be *$42,847 a year* or *$3,571 a month*.

After we account for the expenses that should be lifted off their shoulders by that point, such as mortgage and education/utilities/food for the children, it will give them a standard of living very comparable to what they are enjoying now.

It should be sufficient to sustain two senior citizens with a reasonable degree of comfort, allowing them to be independent of their children. If the children move into their own homes, a room or even two can be rented out, adding to the monthly income.

If the family continues working, saving and investing for a further three years (a total of thirty-three years), they would have a nest egg worth *$1,815,152.02*. A 5 percent dividend yield on that would amount to $90,758 a year in dividends, equivalent to $52,035 in today's dollars ($4,336 a month).

Case Study Three: The Slow Lane – Low-Income Earners

I believe it is possible for even low income earners to save and have financial freedom – if not total financial freedom, then at least partial. It is definitely not easy but with real willpower and willingness to learn, it is *possible*.

For this case study, I shall take the household monthly income from work for the second lowest decile[11] of working households in Singapore, which is $3,907[12]. Of course, the family in this example will have to be even more frugal than the preceding one. Assuming again that there are two breadwinners earning equal amounts, each of them would earn $23,442 a year. After tax reliefs, they would pay virtually no income tax under Singapore's tax regime[13]. Thus $3,907 a month will be treated as the family's net income.

Breakdown of monthly expenses

Mortgage payments for a two-bedroom, new and subsidised HDB (public housing) apartment in Sengkang on a 20-year loan (after government grants)[14]: $665

Utilities: $80 (energy saving bulbs, no air-conditioning. This takes into account regular government subsidies, which are higher for smaller apartments.)

Food and beverage: $969 ($9 per person per day, multiplied by 3.53 persons and 30.5 days a month. This assumes a mean cost of $3 per meal, a dollar lower than in case study two. This will take a great deal of discipline and austerity – often involving very simple meals, bringing lunch boxes from home and your own water instead of buying a drink.)

Transport: $240 (no taxi rides; bus and MRT only)

Internet and mobile phone subscriptions: $80 (no cable TV; use budget prepaid cards)

Allowances to parents (of both spouses): $500

Children's school/ daycare expenses: $500 (for 2 children – this income group typically will not be able to afford private tuition. Their children will need to be more self-reliant and tap other sources of assistance, such as schoolteachers, friends and community welfare organisations. This group also receives very substantial government subsidies for daycare and preschool.)

Insurance: $400 (should go for lower cost plans such as MediShield Life and term life insurance)

Bi-annual holiday: $42 (assuming a destination close by such as Malaysia or Thailand. Estimated total cost $1,000 divided by 24 months.)

Entertainment: $50 (in Singapore, there are numerous leisure options that are free of charge, such as the many museums which allow free entry to citizens and permanent residents, free arts events as well as beautiful parks and gardens. One does not need to spend much to have a great day out.)

Miscellaneous expenses including household repairs: $100

Total monthly expenses: $3,626

Monthly savings = $3,907 – $3,626 = $281

Annual savings = $3,372 for the first 20 years (while paying mortgage) and $11,352 from the 21st year (mortgage fully paid)

Time taken to amass 6-month emergency fund
= 21,756/3,372 = 6.45 years

How long will it take for this family to attain at least partial financial freedom?

Table 4.3: Long-term returns for low-income family (S$)

Year	Annual Investment	Net Return	Total	Remarks
1	0	0	0	Building emergency fund
2	0	0	0	Building emergency fund
3	0	0	0	Building emergency fund
4	0	0	0	Building emergency fund
5	0	0	0	Building emergency fund
6	0	0	0	Building emergency fund
7	1,686.00	101.16	1,787.16	First half of year building emergency fund; able to start investing in second half
8	3,372.00	309.55	5,468.71	
9	3,372.00	530.44	9,371.15	
10	3,372.00	764.59	13,507.74	
11	3,372.00	1,012.78	17,892.53	
12	3,372.00	1,275.87	22,540.40	
13	3,372.00	1,554.74	27,467.40	
14	3,372.00	1,850.35	32,689.49	
15	3,372.00	2,163.69	38,225.18	
16	3,372.00	2,495.83	44,093.01	
17	3,372.00	2,847.90	50,312.91	
18	3,372.00	3,221.09	56,906.00	
19	3,372.00	3,616.68	63,894.69	
20	3,372.00	4,036.00	71,302.69	
21	11,352.00	4,959.28	87,613.97	Mortgage fully paid – can increase savings and investment
22	11,352.00	5,937.96	104,903.93	
23	11,352.00	6,975.36	123,231.28	
24	11,352.00	8,075.00	142,658.28	
25	11,352.00	9,240.62	163,250.89	
26	11,352.00	10,476.17	185,079.07	
27	11,352.00	11,785.86	208,216.93	
28	11,352.00	13,174.14	232,743.07	
29	11,352.00	14,645.70	258,740.77	
30	11,352.00	16,205.57	286,298.34	
31	11,352.00	17,859.02	315,509.36	
32	11,352.00	19,611.68	346,473.04	
33	11,352.00	21,469.50	379,294.54	

After thirty years (including roughly 6.5 years to build up an emergency fund, during which no investment can take place), they would have built up an investment portfolio worth *$286,298.34*. If they can achieve a 5 percent yield on that portfolio, it would garner an *annual passive income of $14,315 ($1,193 a month)*. In *today's dollars*, again assuming a long-term inflation rate of 1.7 percent, that would come up to about $719 *a month*. It is not enough to retire on, but at least it would supplement the family income and perhaps allow at least one of the breadwinners to stop working or reduce working hours and enjoy their golden years.

If the family is able to continue working, saving and investing for another three years, it can amass an investment portfolio worth *$379,294.54*. A dividend yield of 5 percent on this amount generates an annual passive income of $18,965, or $1,580 a month ($906 in today's dollars). If the family is able to rent out a bedroom in their apartment, it will help ease their financial burden and possibly even allow them to retire with a very simple lifestyle.

They would also fully own their home and have a $21,756 emergency fund to cushion them in case of any misfortunes.

If they can devote themselves to achieving a higher than 6 percent long-term compounded rate of return on their investments, they can do better. But this could be an overly risky goal if they are not able to grasp the principles of active investing well enough. It might be better to follow a simple passive investing strategy and be content with 6 percent annual returns.

Certainly I am under no illusion that it would be easy to attain financial freedom, whether in part or in full, if your income is low But I hope that this case study will provide some inspiration, in showing that you can at least shore up your financial foundations; build a certain level of financial security; and, if not achieve total liberation from work, at least have your burden significantly eased.

A Side Street? Alternative Routes To Financial Freedom

With a bit of creativity and open-mindedness, one can sometimes find an alternative route to his destination. Some ingenious Singaporeans, for instance, have capitalised on the cheaper housing and lower cost of living in neighbouring Malaysia. They live in Malaysia and commute across either of two land links to work in Singapore, enjoying a kind of arbitrage between the higher Singapore income and the lower Malaysian costs.

According to Boaz Boon, a senior corporate executive turned entrepreneur, a semi-retired lifestyle is not just for the very rich in Singapore. He sees it as something attainable for most Singaporeans. In fact, based on his estimates, one can live quite comfortably on $1,500 a month — by stretching the dollar across the Causeway, in Malaysia[15]. With $1,500, one can hardly survive in Singapore where the monthly median income from work per household member was $2,699 in 2017. But in Malaysia, that money goes much further.

While great uncertainty hangs over the planned high-speed rail between Singapore and Kuala Lumpur at the time of writing due to a change of government in Malaysia, the Rapid Transit System linking Woodlands in Singapore to Johor Bahru in Malaysia seems set to go ahead. If it does materialise, it will give more Singaporeans the opportunity to "explore the flexibility of living across the Causeway and working in Singapore", says Mr Boon. One does not even need to buy a home in Malaysia; one can just rent, he says. Listings of newly completed terraced houses in developments in Johor Bahru and other parts of Iskandar Malaysia have asking rents of 1,000 to 3,500 Malaysian Ringgit ($339-1,187) a month.

Quite a number of countries have immigration schemes for foreign investors where you can live there long-term with your spouse and children if you commit a reasonable amount of capital to the country. For instance, you would qualify for the Philippines' Special Investor's Resident Visa if you invest a minimum of US$75,000 there[16].

Of course moving to another country means that you leave behind your family and friends. It is not easy to adjust to a completely new environment and rebuild your social circle, but it can also be seen as an adventure. In any case, with the proliferation of budget flights, the world has become a much smaller place.

---

1 Based on the average of households in the second highest decile among resident employed households in Singapore. Source: Department of Statistics Singapore website, accessed 25 May 2018.

2 Assuming that the household income is earned equally by two breadwinners, and there are two children in the family which allows the parents to claim generous tax reliefs.

3 A unit matching this description was transacted at $1,413,000 in Nov 2017. Dover Parkview is a 99-year leasehold property (lease beginning in 1993). The unit can comfortably accommodate a family of up to five, and the 74 years remaining on the leasehold land tenure is more than enough to last the lifetime of the parents and most of the lifetime of the children. The monthly mortgage instalment is calculated based on the following assumptions: 15 percent downpayment, 20-year floating rate loan at a rate of the 8-month fixed deposit rate plus 1.45 percent, which works out to 1.65 percent at time of writing. But I have done my sums using a 2.65 percent interest rate to capture the risk of rising interest rates.

4   It is important to note that cars in Singapore are among the most expensive in the world due to an extremely heavy taxation structure, notably the Additional Registration Fee which can be up to 180 percent of the Open Market Value of the car, and the Certificate of Entitlement which is a permit to use the car for 10 years and priced by auction usually for tens of thousands of dollars.

5   A 6 percent compounded return is very achievable if you follow sound investing principles. Many REITs in Singapore yield over 6 percent a year in dividends alone. Many stocks yield 4 percent or more, and if you buy a well-run business, it can grow and provide capital gain and total returns far in excess of 6 percent. According to SGX My Gateway, even the Straits Times Index exchange-traded funds (ETFs) produced an 8.4 percent compounded annual gain (including dividends) over the 10-year period ending Feb 2014.

6   As of May 2018, most REITs in Singapore were yielding more than 5 percent a year, with many offering 6 percent or more. There were also a good number of stocks that could produce 5 percent or higher yields quite consistently, such as Hotung Investment Holdings, Avi-Tech and QAF, as well as business trusts such as Accordia Golf Trust.

7   Department of Statistics Singapore website, accessed 31 Jan 2018.

8   ibid.

9   In Singaporean parlance, a four-room Housing and Development Board (HDB) apartment is actually a three-bedroom apartment. I selected an apartment with these characteristics as I felt it represents quite well a reasonably comfortable, middle-of-the-road choice for a middle-class family. Yishun is neither the cheapest nor the most expensive of estates; the floor area of 108 sq m is very comfortable for an average household size of 3.53 persons. In Jan 2018, there was a resale transaction of $375,000 for such an apartment.

The loan repayment calculation was based on 20 percent downpayment, a 20-year loan tenure and an interest rate of 2.65 percent. To be conservative (as interest rates are currently very low by historical standards), I added a full percentage point to the DBS interest rate for a floating rate loan package as of 1 Feb 2018, which was 1.65 percent (source: DBS website). The computation of monthly repayment was done using the DBS Loan Calculator at https://www.dbs.com.sg/personal/landing/loans/homeloans/calculate/loan-hdb.html?pid=sg-dbs-lp-loans-calculate-loans-textlinkhomeloanrepayment-hdb

A family could get a home much more cheaply if they opted for a new apartment with heavy subsidy from the HDB rather than buy a resale apartment at open market prices. The disadvantage is that they will have to wait for the apartment to be ready and they might not get their first-choice location.

10 There is currently no tax on dividends or capital gains in Singapore.

11 A decile is a slice of ten percent of a population, part of a ranking of the population according to a certain variable such as income. Thus the lowest decile of a household income distribution would be the bottom ten percent. The second lowest decile would be the second lowest 10 percent, and so on.

12 "Key Household Income Trends, 2016", Department of Statistics Singapore.

13 In Singapore, taxes apply only after the first $20,000 of annual taxable income. Males who have performed mandatory national service receive a tax relief of $1,500-5,000, and even their wives get a $750 break. Couples get a $4,000 break for each child, which they can share between themselves. Working mothers are also eligible for tax relief of 15-25 percent of earned income for each child, depending on birth order. Source: Inland Revenue Authority website, 23 May 2018.

14 The HDB press release "HDB Launches 8,230 Flats in Nov 2017 BTO and SBF Exercise" (http://www.hdb.gov.sg/cs/infoweb/press-releases/bto-nov-launch-14112017-) states that a three-room (two-bedroom) flat in the non-mature estate of Sengkang could cost as little as $103,000 if the buyers qualified for government grants (Additional CPF Housing Grant and Special CPF Housing Grant) of $75,000 in total. For our case study I will assume a more conservative price of $138,000 to factor in the possibility that the buyer did not qualify to receive that large an amount of grant or that he chose a slightly more expensive unit. I shall also assume a loan from HDB with 10 percent down payment and a loan tenure of 20 years. The HDB interest rate was 2.6 percent as at 2 Feb 2018. I shall not adjust this rate as it is pegged to CPF Ordinary Account interest rate plus 0.1 percent, and CPF interest rate is stable and likely to remain so.

15 "Lure of a comfortable, semi-retired lifestyle at just $1,500 a month", Cecilia Chow, Edgeprop Singapore, 10 June 2018 https://www.edgeprop.sg/property-news/lure-comfortable-semi-retired-lifestyle-just-1500-month?utm_source=newsletter&utm_medium=email&utm_campaign=SPOTLIGHT&utm_source=Subs+%2B+Agent+%28Merged%29&utm_campaign=7920b10df2-EMAIL_CAMPAIGN_2018_06_011&utm_medium=email&utm_term=0_b55410cdf5-7920b10df2-3269265

16 According to the Philippine Embassy website. Accessed 20 June 2018.

CHAPTER 5

HOW AND WHAT TO INVEST IN

Strangely enough, it was during my national service days that I became interested in investing in general, and the stock market in particular. It was 1976, and I was serving as an infantry officer in the People's Defence Force (PDF) in Pulau Tekong, an island off Singapore that's used for the training of full-time national servicemen and reservists who had completed their full-time national service.

In our Camp II on Pulau Tekong, the reservists we were retraining had served as military police, drivers, medics, clerks and cooks. We received a new batch every month and our duty was to reshape them into infantry soldiers, ready for combat should they be called up. Their four-week course was akin to a compressed Basic Military Training (BMT) course that every able-bodied young Singaporean had to go through at the start of his two or two-and-a-half years of national service.

In our free time, after the training each day, my Officer Commanding, Tommie Goh, and I would mingle with the reservists and discuss various things over coffee or a beer. Some of the reservist officers were active investors and they would share how well they had done in the stock market. In 1976, the market had gone through a bad patch since the OPEC oil crisis in 1973 and was just beginning to recover after plumbing new lows in 1975. It presented an opportunity and the smart money was moving in to ride the upturn.

I was learning from these investor reservists, as my background was in science, especially physics, and mathematics. As an officer, I was drawing a reasonable allowance of about $550 per month and, after making contributions to my home and personal expenses, there was about $250 to spare each month. One day, I decided to take the plunge and open an account with Tsang and Ong Stockbrokers. Then, I bought what I thought was the cheapest stock in the market, a company called Hytex. Its share price was about 30 cents and I became the proud owner of 1,000 shares of Hytex, a maker of polypropylene bags.

Unfortunately, the investment did not work out well. Hytex kept losing money and was eventually threatened with liquidation after a period of suspension in trading. Luckily for me, an Indonesian group moved in to take over the shell in 1983 and inject its own diverse businesses into Hytex. So Hytex survived. It is now trading as Tuan Sing Holdings. Hytex shareholders though received only a wee bit of Tuan Sing shares. It was a bad start in investing for me, but it was also a good lesson learnt.

Investing is not about watching price action in the market and taking a plunge into anything moving up rapidly or which looks cheap in an absolute sense.

I began to read the *Business Times* and to learn more about the economy and business in general. I found companies and the stock market to be fascinating. The economy was regaining its vibrancy and there was a lot to learn. I read and invested selectively.

Upon completion of my national service at the end of 1976, I reapplied to the *Business Times* (BT), which was part of The Straits Times Press, for a job as a reporter. They had kept the position for me in reserve from July 1974, when I had first knocked on their doors after finishing my science degree in the University of Singapore (now called the National University of Singapore). BT was happy to take me in immediately, in January 1977, but again I asked for a deferment for my start date as I wanted to do some travelling.

I finally joined BT in August 1977 as a rookie reporter on the Companies Desk. By then, the founding editor, Tan Sai Siong, had left and Scotsman Roy Mackie was in the saddle. Roy was happy to let me work on the Companies Desk, which covered listed companies and the stock market. My passion for the affairs of companies and the market allowed me to progress rapidly to the number two position on the Desk and, later, as Companies Editor.

I continued to invest, but of course, keeping a log of my investments and avoiding a conflict of interests between my writing and investing. Meeting corporate chiefs and interviewing them on business strategies made me more aware of the ups and downs of business and the companies involved. I learnt more about how to analyse companies and to decide what made a good investment at any point of time. I was into value investing.

WHAT SHOULD I INVEST IN?

There are all kinds of assets that one can invest in, from stocks to bonds, real estate to gold, art to wine.

Those who opt for bonds usually do relatively better than bank depositors as bank deposits are low-risk, low reward. For bond holders, the risks are somewhat higher and the rewards too. Bonds should keep up with inflation as the years go by, given their higher interest yields than bank deposits. But bond holders have to ensure the bonds are linked to entities that do not eventually default. Do note that bonds are not an investment *in* a business; they are more like lending money to a business.

Property investment can be a viable option and do as well as stock market investing. But the asset classes are very different. Property is a long-term game and it is important to understand what drives prices in a particular city or country. There may be tax benefits or reliefs for property owners and some locations may be especially attractive. These factors are important but the underlying demographics must be right and demand has to be rising over the years as the population grows. Chapter 6 covers Property and REITs.

In my opinion stocks are one of the best asset classes to invest in. *Thus this book focuses mainly on stocks (ordinary shares).* Unlike bonds, stocks are direct investments in a business and represent the best way in risk/reward terms to build wealth steadily while participating in the growth of a business. This is not to say that bonds cannot make a great investment, but I like stocks as they give ordinary people the opportunity to experience what I call "the magic of business" – the power to grow one dollar into two, ten or even a hundred dollars. We have witnessed such multiplying of capital in outstanding businesses like Coca-Cola, Google, or here in Singapore, Venture Corporation[1].

Of course we cannot expect such phenomenal returns all the time, nor should we take on more risk than we can tolerate in order to pursue such returns. Even a 7 percent-a-year return, compounded over ten years, will almost double our money and beat bank interest rates hands down (do read up online on the magic of compounding and the rule of 72).

I also prefer direct purchases of stocks to putting money in unit trusts (mutual funds) as the latter is an indirect way to participate in businesses, and takes control out of your hands. Your profits are also reduced by the fees charged by the fund manager. *An alternative, however, is to buy into low-fee exchange-traded funds (ETFs) as part of a passive investing strategy.* Details are given in this chapter.

Here are some of the most important principles on investing that I have learned and/or developed along my forty-two-year investment journey:

CORE PRINCIPLES OF INVESTING
Combine Common Sense With Critical Thinking

This combination is important because, without critical thinking, "Common Sense" can easily lapse into common stupidity – mindlessly believing something just because the crowd believes it. A fine example would be the popular fallacy that a stock is cheap simply because its price has fallen, or is expensive simply because of its rising stock price. If you had applied the first part of that nonsense to Chartered Semiconductor in Singapore, you would have suffered a grievous loss; if you had used the second in relation to Apple Inc, you would have missed out on a life-changing opportunity.

Cultivate Emotional Discipline

It may seem strange to give emotions such prominence in a discussion on investing, something that most people would associate with cold logic and numbers. However, as mentioned in Chapter 1 of this book, an investor's worst enemy is often himself. The reason why most people buy high and sell low is that they cannot control the twin beasts of greed and fear within their human psyche. Even normally unemotional people will experience great waves of greed or fear when profits beckon or losses erupt – it is a part of the human survival mechanism. Therefore always bear in mind Benjamin Graham's belief: *that financial risk lies not only in our investments or the economy, but in ourselves.*

Therefore *if you truly desire to succeed as an investor, you will have to invest effort in cultivating emotional discipline.* This is more difficult for some than for others and, indeed, it can be a long and frustrating journey. But it is also a fruitful one, and if you are prepared to walk every step, you will get there eventually.

The Concept Of Mr Market

This personification of the market is one of the most wonderful concepts from Benjamin Graham. It represents the market as a highly temperamental, even manic-depressive, individual. When he is in a hyper-exuberant mood, he will sell to you (or buy from you) stocks at ridiculously high prices. When he is mired in depression, he will sell to you all that he has at garage-sale prices or even less.

We will benefit from challenging this depiction of Mr Market to some extent. In truth, most of the time the market is actually quite efficient at pricing its stocks. It may lean towards being overly optimistic or overly pessimistic on most days, but these emotional states are usually not extreme and stock prices reflect the fundamental strengths of the underlying business fairly well most of the time.

Mr Market is more stable than most people think. But certainly he does sometimes become irrationally elated or unduly despondent, as the market is driven by the powerful pushes and pulls of crowd psychology. This is when we can get unusually good deals selling to him or buying from him.

Invest As Part Of A Holistic Financial Plan

Never lose sight of the bigger picture. While investing is probably the sexiest and most exciting of our financial endeavours, remember that it is just one part of a financial framework that keeps us on solid ground. Make sure you apportion your resources sensibly between savings (always maintaining an emergency fund of six months' expenses or more), insurance and investment. The six months' expenses should include insurance premiums and property mortgage payments.

Financial plans are for the long term and they require persistence and discipline. Once you have enough cash to pull the family through without any income for six months, and your insurance policies are in place and adequate, you are ready to invest. Do not rush into investments the moment you have some spare cash.

[A small caveat: Multimillionaires may not need health or life insurance as they can self-insure with their vast resources.]

Know What You Are Doing

Before you invest, do your homework. In school, if you didn't do your homework, you might have gotten a scolding from the teacher or be made to stand outside the class. In investing, not doing your homework is likely to have much more serious repercussions.

My friend Wan Hsin-hun has astutely observed that some people spend more time researching into what to have for lunch than into a stock transaction that costs a hundred or even a thousand times more.[2] Perhaps such behaviour stems from our upbringing – many of us grew up being told that we must work hard at our studies, work hard at our jobs to make money, but not many were told that we need to work hard at *managing* our money once we have earned it. It is a shame that most people never even come close to fulfilling the immense potential power of the money they make – or worse, they throw away their hard-earned savings due to their lazy or flippant attitude towards money.

Don't make that mistake. Invest time not only in your job, but spend a bit of your time on the art and science of investing as well. Dedicate an hour on your day off to reading a company's annual report. Cut down on Korean drama serials or English Premier League highlights and squeeze in 30 minutes on a weeknight to peruse the business news or an investment website or book.

So how much technical knowledge do you need to be a good investor? You should understand the basics of the industry that the company is in, the basics of its own particular business, and the basics of accounting – the essentials of the profit and loss statement, balance sheet and cashflow statement. Don't worry even if you have zero accounting knowledge to start with – *just pick it up piece by piece*. There is a wealth of websites, like Investopedia, that explain these terms in an easy-to-understand manner.

You don't need to delve too deeply into the technical details. Just seek to achieve a fundamental understanding of the company's situation and financial health. For instance, if debt is high relative to assets and the company's earnings are barely enough to cover interest payments, then your Common Sense will tell you that the company can easily get into trouble if it suffers a downturn. Also, if receivables are building up much faster than revenue, ask yourself what can it mean? Perhaps their customers are unable, or unwilling, to pay.

Basic due diligence on a company before you put your money in will comprise reading at least its latest annual report and the latest financial statements (it could be quarterly or half-yearly results announcements). Also useful are interviews with the chairman or CEO in the media, articles about the company and the industry, and analyst reports. But always take all these with a pinch of salt, and do your own critical, independent thinking.

If the results of your investments matter to you, then put in the time and do your homework.

Can You Trust These Guys?

If a stranger were to come up to you in the street and say "Hey, you wanna put ten thousand dollars in my company?", we would probably quicken our steps to escape him as soon as possible.

But when we hear about a sexy business on the stock market, many of us pump very substantial sums of our hard-earned cash into it without even pausing to ask ourselves whether we can trust the people who run the company.

As Benjamin Graham wrote, "Investment is most intelligent when it is most business-like." So treat buying a stock as entering into a business deal. Before parting with your precious capital, surely you should take some time to size up your prospective business partners and get a sense of their character and intentions. *Only when you have a high degree of assurance that they are people of integrity should you put your capital in their hands.*

So how can you tell if the head honchos can be trusted? Like investing in general, it is a combination of art and science. You should try to meet them face-to-face, look them in the eye and ask them some probing questions about their business. The manner in which they respond, both verbally and non-verbally, will give you a few signals about their character. Some intuition may be needed here; even though intuition may be flawed, one cannot deny that sometimes it is an important guide in life. And it can be honed.

You can get these opportunities in different settings. The most common one is at the company annual general meeting (AGM). The problem with AGMs is that only shareholders can attend; an approach that many of my friends use is to buy the minimum amount of shares (it could cost as little as $40 including transaction costs) just to be able to attend the meeting. Some companies hold investor open days that even non-shareholders can attend; others may even be willing to arrange a meeting with you to answer your queries, especially if you can bring a group of investors so that their time is well-spent.

However, meeting and communicating with the firm's leaders can only tell you so much. Ultimately, *actions speak louder* than any pretty words or warm smiles – so judge them first and foremost by their *actions*. In particular, do they have *a track record* of giving smaller shareholders their fair share, i.e. do they pay out a fair proportion of their earnings in the form of dividends? Of course it's understandable if they do not pay out 100 percent of profits as it is good for a business to retain some earnings for future expansion, capital expenditure or just as a buffer in bad times. But if they are paying only 20 percent or less, do they have a good reason?

It is crucial that investors be not satisfied with merely sweet-talk and heartwarming promises from companies. You must learn to demand of them, to quote Tom Cruise's character in *Jerry Maguire*, "Show me the money!"

Certainly there are listed firms that commit accounting fraud and embezzlement. But there is also no end of ways that corporate boards can short-change shareholders *without* breaking the law. One is to pay the directors nice, fat fees but distribute only crumbs and peanuts to its shareholders.

Remember that minority shareholders, with a non-controlling stake in a company, are susceptible to abuse or oppression by the majority or controlling shareholders. This is because the small shareholder has little say in the running of the company's affairs. Though he has legal avenues to pursue a grievance against controlling shareholders if he feels oppressed, the fact is that most of us do not have the time or money to seek redress. Thus it is best to avoid the need to do so by investing our hard-earned money only in companies that are run by honest and honourable people.

Read more about minority oppression and other misconduct by listed companies in Chapter 9.

I generally trust only listed companies (listcos) that have paid dividends fairly for at least five years. This track record is important, as only time can tell whether someone is honest. Some listcos treat shareholders well for two or three years, and all of a sudden slash dividends for no good reason. Their end-game could be to cause the share price to crash so that they can attempt to take back shares on the cheap from dispirited minority investors (in a general offer, for example) and privatise the company – yet another way to short-change the man on the street.

Thus it is by and large not advisable to subscribe to initial public offerings (IPOs) or buy recently listed stocks from the open market. New listcos have no track record in terms of how they treat shareholders.

Other questions worth asking before you invest: has the company or any of its directors ever been caught or investigated for any unsavoury actions, e.g. insider trading or questionable accounting practices? Has any director ever been involved in a dubious corporate manoeuvre, for instance placing out new shares at a big discount to a third party without good justification, or attempting to grab a company's shares on the cheap with a general offer during a transient downturn? Has the company been open and forthcoming with information when adverse events occur?

When you wade into the stock market, you are entering the world of finance and big money. Human greed abounds and all the evils that accompany it – thus it is a bit like entering a sea of sharks. Therefore, as the boxing referees always say at the start of a fight, protect yourself at all times.

Earlier in the book I spoke of the stock market as a way to experience "the magic of business". But this is only possible with a company run by honest, honourable people who desire to do right by the shareholders who provided them the capital to grow their business. Thankfully, there are such businesses and good folks around – we just need to search hard to find them.

Are These Guys Capable?

Integrity is not the only thing needed to make a listed firm a good investment – the competence and talent of the bosses matter a great deal, too.

When I was adjunct professor at SIM University, I conducted research on Singapore companies to suss out their success factors. The study, which covered more than 30 enterprises listed on the Singapore Exchange, truly underlined for me how crucial the quality of leadership is. I found a common thread running through the leaders of winning companies, which was that they were all gifted problem-solvers.

You can assess the problem-solving abilities of corporate leaders by observing how they respond to a wide range of challenges, from political instability in their markets to the emergence of fierce competitors to public relations disasters.

In a world of accelerating change, *the ability to adapt* is more vital than ever. Technology and globalisation can disrupt even the most established businesses. A fine example of an adaptable company is Memtech International, a global components solution provider serving, among others, the automotive, medical and consumer electronics industries. Once one of the world's top keypad makers for mobile phones, they ran into severe difficulty in 2011 when touchscreen smartphones became popular and traditional mobile phones went into terminal decline. Memtech slumped into two years of losses. But they cudgelled their brains and came up with ways to use their expertise to make different products that were in demand. Eventually they became a much sought-after component maker for major automotive suppliers such as Magna and Lear, as well as world-class consumer electronics brands like Beats, Bose and JBL.

Adaptability is part of problem-solving, and also part of an individual's overall *dynamism*. Judge for yourself whether the board of directors is dynamic – positive in attitude, energetic and full of new ideas. If you as a shareholder want your company to thrive or even survive, you will want it to be run by individuals who are always seeking to do better, and trying to find new ways of thinking and doing. You don't want executive directors who are static or complacent, and just happy to muddle along. Or non-executive directors who don't seem to be engaged and are just sitting on the board to collect fees.

Be careful, though, of some leaders who seem to be buzzing with new ideas but are really just wildly trying out new lines of business that they have little to no competence in, just because their existing business is in decline. For instance, if an oil palm grower suddenly decides to diversify into women's lingerie and video games, you should ask some serious questions about whether the bosses know what they are doing.

When you study a company, do read the profiles of directors and top management in the annual report – their qualifications and work experience – and make a judgement on how qualified they are to perform their role.

If you have an opportunity to watch or read an interview with them, or see them in action at a company AGM, you will be able to assess other qualities such as their communication skills and EQ – surely also significant to their effectiveness as leaders. Of course there are some highly effective CEOs who do not speak well at all – it is just one of the factors in the equation.

Decide On Your Investment Approach

What approach is best for you? Should it be active, passive or both? The classification of investing approaches is a very tricky affair, but a good starting point is that there are two broad approaches to investing in stocks: active and passive.

The active approach is one where you are regularly involved in the research, selection and monitoring of the stocks in your portfolio, spending a considerable amount of time (it could be anything from seven to fifty hours a week, or even more). The active investor seeks superior returns through this diligent application of his mind and his time.

The passive approach, on the other hand, is a system that requires very little time or thinking on the part of the investor, who simply applies a sound formula and follows it mechanically. If the formula is indeed sound (and you must make sure that it is logically sound, and not just *nice-sounding*), this highly low-maintenance approach can also turn out to be successful.

I will just share a couple of formulas here. Probably the most popular is dollar-cost averaging (DCA). This entails investing a fixed dollar amount at set intervals (usually monthly, but it can also be quarterly or even yearly) into a set of stocks (usually an index fund or exchange-traded fund that tracks an index, such as the S & P 500 in the US); or a regular share savings or RSS plan offered by banks and stockbrokers. The latter may allow you to invest in individual stocks or exchange-traded funds (ETFs) in small amounts periodically. Make sure transaction costs are not too high as they will otherwise eat into your profits over time.

If you prefer to invest in funds rather than individual stocks, it would probably be best to select *passively* managed funds such as exchange-traded funds (ETFs) as they charge much lower fees than *actively* managed mutual funds or unit trusts. Sadly, the majority of actively managed funds often underperform their index benchmarks while charging you relatively high fees. In fact, S & P Dow Jones reported in 2016 that a stunning 99 percent of actively managed US equity funds sold in Europe failed to beat the S & P 500 Index over the previous ten years, while only two in every 100 global equity funds had outperformed the S & P Global 1200 in the same period[3].

Why do actively managed funds underperform? There are many contributing factors. One reason, naturally, is the higher fees they charge, which erode returns to investors. Another is structural problems, for instance the fact that once a fund grows to a certain size, the rewards are fat for the managers and they become afraid to rock the boat – they then tend to just play safe and more or less follow the benchmark. Once they do so, it is almost guaranteed that the fund will underperform in terms of returns to the investor, as it can only match the performance of the index *before* the managers deduct their high fees. When a fund is successful, new investors and capital pour in, often resulting in more cash in the manager's hands than there are good opportunities available. He may put the money into the stocks he's already bought but they may have become overvalued. He may research new stocks to put money into but might end up following more companies than he is able to handle[4].

DCA is mathematically quite a logical method. When stock prices are higher, you buy fewer units or shares; when prices are lower, you buy more units or shares. This is because the exact same dollar amount is going in every month or quarter. The result is that your average cost will be lower than the average market price over time. (Ideally, you should invest in an index that is diversified across industries, such as the S & P 500, the Straits Times Index or the Hang Seng Index, so that any long-term decline in a particular industry will not hurt you badly. Additionally, high-quality indices such as the ones just mentioned are made up of mostly well-managed businesses, which are likely to survive at least the duration of your lifetime.)

A simple illustration of DCA

In January, the market price is $2 a share.
You buy $100 worth, receiving 100/2 = 50 shares.

In February, the market crashes and price is down to $1 a share. You buy $100 worth, receiving 100/1 = 100 shares (buying twice as many shares when price halves).

What is the average market price over the two months?
(2+1)/2 = $1.50 a share

The average cost of your purchases?
200/(50+100) =200/150
=$1.33 a share

Another technique is value averaging (VA). This method takes into consideration the expected rate of return of your investment. Accordingly, investors contribute to their portfolios in such a way that the portfolio balance (total value of portfolio) increases by a set amount in each time period, regardless of market fluctuations. Consequently, in periods when prices rise, the investor puts in a smaller dollar amount; when prices fall, he does the opposite.

For instance, let's say your portfolio balance is now $5,000 and the goal is for the portfolio to grow by $300 every month. After one month, the market has risen and your portfolio balance has grown by $150 to $5,150. Thus you would contribute only $300-$150 = $150 that month to raise your portfolio value to $5,300. A problem with this method is that you might at some point not have the funds to make up shortfalls in portfolio value. There may be times too, such as during a cataclysmic market crash as in 2008/09, when it would take a huge injection of funds to follow this formula. In such cases, you could perhaps just inject the amount that you can afford. Such situations are extraordinary and, after a few years at most, the market usually returns to normal.

Like dollar-cost averaging, VA enables investors to buy more when stocks are cheap – but in a more pronounced way.

While no formula can guarantee satisfactory returns, there is significant research to suggest that DCA and VA give you a good chance of achieving them. For instance, *Straits Times* journalist Aaron Low found that a dollar-cost averaging investment of $1 m spread out over ten years (June 2006 to June 2016) in the Straits Times Index exchange-traded fund (ETF) in Singapore produced a portfolio value of $1.29 m (inclusive of dividends).[5]

There was also a 2012 empirical paper by mutual fund giant Vanguard that ran simulations of DCA with a 60 percent stock and 40 percent bond allocation in rolling ten-year periods. The simulation was done in three markets: the US, Britain and Australia. In the case of the US, the study relied on data stretching over an incredibly long period: 1926–2011. Using a sum of US$1 m invested in monthly instalments over *one year*, it computed an average ending portfolio value of US$2,395,824 after *ten years* in the US market. In other words, US$1 m injected over twelve months into the market would have grown, on average, to about US$2.4 m after ten years during the period under study.[6]

It is worth noting that this paper found that investing your money in one lump sum outperformed a twelve-month dollar-cost averaging approach approximately 67 percent of the time in the US. Interestingly, it also noted that this incidence of outperformance was roughly the same even with a 100 percent equity (stock) portfolio or a 100 percent bond portfolio. In the case of a 60-40 blend of stocks and bonds, the average ending portfolio value was US$2,450,264, or 2.3 percent higher than for the twelve-month DCA.

The paper, however, does acknowledge that "risk-averse investors may be less concerned about averages than they are about worst-case scenarios, as well as the potential feelings of regret that would occur if a lump-sum investment (LSI) were made immediately prior to a market decline." These emotional considerations are very real. The paper also discovered that decreases in portfolio values occurred more frequently for LSI than DCA investors, and the average falls in portfolio value were also much steeper for the former.

You must really do some reflection and ask yourself, honestly, on a scale of 1 to 10, how much volatility you can stomach. If you score 4 and below, then probably the DCA approach is best for you.

I would like to highlight one final consideration from the Vanguard study: it finds that the longer the time periods over which you spread out your DCA, the higher the probability of underperformance. In the case of a thirty-six-month dollar-cost averaging, it trailed behind a lump sum investment in 90 percent of the rolling ten-year spans in America. A more recent paper by Vanguard, in 2016, suggests a DCA of no more than twelve months.[7]

If you wish, you can carry out a combination of active and passive approaches: allocate *x* percent of your investible funds to active strategies and the remainder to passive.

The key is to work out an approach that fits your tolerance for volatility, target returns and the amount of time and effort you are willing to put in. Personally, I believe it is well worth investing time and effort to pursue at least a partially active strategy.

How Risk-Averse Are You?

Make an honest assessment. We need to look at risk objectively, with our rational mind and not our emotions. Be clear that *risk runs across a spectrum*, say from 0 to 10. Thus, if you are risk-averse, you do not need to choose a 0 – you can try a 3 or 4. Some people see the stock market as monolithic – as though every stock on the market scores a 9 or 10 for risk. Far from it. An established business run by trusted business veterans with a strong competitive 'moat', lots of cash and no debt on the balance sheet is far less risky than one that is mediocre, run by unknown Johnny-come-latelys, and has little cash and heavy debt.

Risk can also be managed by diversification: spreading your eggs out over different stocks, geographies and industries. When I say geographies, I don't necessarily mean buying stocks listed in different countries. You could buy stocks of companies listed in only one country, but which do business in different countries and continents. That too is a form of diversification.

However, be careful not to *over-diversify*. If you spread your resources too thin, you will miss out on the substantial benefits of "the magic of business": if one of your stocks turns out to be the next Netflix, and your original investment only made up 0.5 percent of your portfolio value, you won't see much impact on your overall wealth even if the stock returned 1,000 percent.

If you are a seasoned investor with proven skills in assessing a business' intrinsic value, then it would make sense for you to run a concentrated portfolio of five to fifteen stocks. If you would like the comfort of greater spreading of risk, then a basket of twenty to thirty stocks would make sense. But as Charlie Munger said, "How could one man know enough [to] own a flowing portfolio of 150 securities and always outperform the averages? That would be a considerable stump."[8]

Assess risk on a *portfolio* basis rather than only on a stock-by-stock basis. For instance, if your overall risk tolerance is a 5, you could buy a couple of level 7 stocks. Just don't make them too big a part of your portfolio, and balance them with a couple of 3s and 4s. If you can still sleep well at night with that package of assets, then you're alright.

By the way, risk tolerance can also be built up with cultivation. If you become a calmer, more objective, bolder person, your risk tolerance could rise with time.

A little food for thought: seeking to live life at a risk level of 0 or 1 is probably a recipe for mediocrity or even failure.

Find The Asset Allocation That's Best For You

Should I put 100 percent of my investible assets in stocks? The orthodox thinking is that an investor should diversify between different asset classes, a popular model being 25-75 percent in stocks and 25-75 percent in bonds. The idea is to smooth out volatility (which is not equal to risk, as I explain below). But this popular belief does not always hold, as there are times when stocks and bonds move almost in lockstep.

It is also a popular belief that bonds are less risky than stocks, so a person with a lower risk tolerance is typically advised to put more money in bonds than in stocks, for instance a 60-40 or 75-25 split.

First, I should counsel that it is a misconception that bonds are always less risky than stocks. In the case of the former, it really depends on the credit-worthiness and resilience of the bond issuer. A US government bond comes with virtually zero default risk as the US government can always print more money to repay bond holders. But a corporate bond often carries a real risk of default, even when the credit rating is high. The rating agencies can often get it wrong, such as in the period leading up to the 2008/2009 subprime crisis in the US when rating agencies stamped high grades onto mortgage-backed securities (complex derivative investments) which were actually linked to highly risky property loans to weak borrowers. These securities ultimately turned out to be toxic, causing billions of dollars in losses around the world.

One has to do proper due diligence on the issuer of a bond, just as one would a listed company before one buys its stock. This book does not focus on bonds, but many of the criteria for evaluating the investment-worthiness of a company's stock are also relevant to whether its bonds are a good investment. For instance, methods of assessing the integrity and capability of the directors, risk factors to the business as well as the resilience of the earnings versus the level of indebtedness on the company's balance sheet. Once you determine the level of risk, ask yourself whether the yield on the bond is more than sufficient to compensate you for taking that risk.

The fallacy that bonds are always safer than stocks has led some investors, even high net-worth ones, to plough large portions of their assets into a bond (sometimes on the advice of their bankers) that later went bust. Sadly, even millionaires can fail to follow the Common Sense principle of doing their homework when it comes to their investments. A case that comes to mind is that of the Swiber bonds in Singapore which went into default. Many wealthy investors blindly followed the advice of their bankers to buy these bonds, without a proper understanding of the risk factors involved in the offshore and marine sector which Swiber was involved in. This sector is heavily affected by the price of oil, which had looked vulnerable to profound technological changes (notably the 'fracking' technology which allowed the US to become a major oil producer, greatly boosting global supply); and also geopolitical shifts, such as tensions between OPEC members causing the cartel to become disunited and ineffective. True enough, the price of oil tumbled and the offshore and marine sector was left reeling, including Swiber.

Therefore some bonds are actually very risky and, conversely, some stocks can actually be less risky than these bonds. For instance, the stock of a company with a dominant market position, diversified business and strong balance sheet. Of course risk also depends on whether you buy the stock at a big discount to fair value, exactly at fair value or above fair value.

Thus we should avoid simplistic thinking and question the popular ideologies in investment. To me, it is not necessarily very risky to have 100 percent of one's assets in stocks if one has sufficient diversification and has bought into well-managed businesses at sizeable discounts to fair value.

No doubt, some diversification into the right bonds can help reduce portfolio volatility and make investing less stressful as the huge movements in stock prices during crisis times can be mentally very difficult to handle for some individuals, especially inexperienced investors. *You must understand yourself, your strengths and your weaknesses.* If you cannot stomach large short-term swings in your net worth, then do not expose yourself too much to stocks. Find the threshold that you are comfortable with, such as 20 or 30 percent. The rest of your money can be held in cash or lower-risk bonds. Try to build yourself up psychologically over time and strengthen your ability to analyse risk objectively, putting aside emotion. In time to come, you may be able to handle a higher level of risk, at which time you can increase your allocation to stocks.

In any case, it is good to set aside about 15-30 percent of investible assets (on top of your emergency fund) in cash. This can be a great 'opportunity fund' that allows you to grab bargains in the stock market during the inevitable crisis periods.

Perhaps investors with less than seven years' experience would do well to tread relatively lightly, for instance by not putting more than 30 to 40 percent of their assets in stocks. This is to give them time to experience the natural swings of the market, especially crises, and learn how to handle them without excessive stress. Do not bite off more than you can chew.

Don't Fear Risk – Manage It

The stock market is like the sea – it can be placid on some days, rough on others, and utterly violent at times. Many people see the volatile nature of stock prices and come to the conclusion that the stock market is a very risky place. But *volatility is not equal to risk*. This is a very difficult concept to truly internalise (because we have been conditioned by the incredibly popular fallacy that equates the two), but a crucial one if you hope to succeed as an investor. So do make an effort to reflect on it.

Volatility can be likened to the change on the complexion of the sea, whether it is calm, choppy or heaving in massive waves. But risk from a long-term perspective is akin to changes in the substance of the sea. If you invest in a well-run, adaptable business with durable competitive advantage, it is like a sea whose substance does not change easily. Yes, due to the adrenaline-fuelled (sometimes manic-depressive) nature of the stock market, the complexion of the sea may change in dramatic ways from day to day. But the intrinsic value of the well-run business (the substance of the sea) remains consistent, and it is this *intrinsic value* that has the greatest say in your final outcomes. This is because after periods of irrational market emotions – either bullish or bearish – subside, objectivity returns and *stock price usually will converge with, or at least move towards, intrinsic value in the long run.*

Thus, risk is defined by Warren Buffett as the probability that an investor will have less purchasing power in the future than she does now, as a result of her investment. As Buffett views all stock purchases through the lens of long-term investment, his idea of the future here is surely at least twenty years (although to most mere mortals like us, five or ten years can also be quite safely viewed as long-term).

Volatility is only equal to risk if you are unwilling or unable to hold your stock for the long term. This underscores the vital importance of keeping at least a six-month emergency fund which will give you the holding power that divorces volatility from risk.

An instructive case would be that of Venture Corporation, one of Singapore's finest listed firms. The stock traded as high as $16.50 in 2007, plunged to $4.05 during the Global Financial Crisis of 2009, recovered to $9.42 that same year, then spent most of the next seven years within the $7-$9+ range. From Feb 2016 it began a steep climb to reach $24.30 on 19 Jan 2018.

Tremendous volatility in stock price. But underneath that was a fundamentally very sound and steady company run by brilliant people who had what it takes to survive and thrive in the tough world of business. Thus the risk was really far lower than the swings in the share price.

Also consider this: throughout the entire period mentioned above (in fact since listing in 1992), Venture has paid a dividend every single year – including a substantial 50 cents per share in each of the crisis-hit years of 2008 and 2009.

The words of Warren Buffett in Berkshire Hathaway's 2014 letter to shareholders are, as always, illuminating and compelling (emphasis in italics and comments in square brackets are mine):

"It is true, of course, that owning equities for a day or a week or a year is far riskier (in both nominal and purchasing-power terms) than leaving funds in cash-equivalents. That is relevant to certain investors – say, investment banks – whose viability can be threatened by declines in asset prices and which might be forced to sell securities during depressed markets.

Additionally, any party that might have meaningful near-term needs for funds should keep appropriate sums in Treasuries [bonds and other debt obligations of the US government] or insured bank deposits.

"For the great majority of investors, however, *who can – and should – invest with a multi-decade horizon, quotational declines* [falls in the market price of stocks on a day-to-day basis] are unimportant. Their focus should remain fixed on attaining significant gains in purchasing power over their investing lifetime. For them, *a diversified equity* [stock] *portfolio, bought over time, will prove far less risky than dollar-based securities* [securities like bonds, whose value rests in large part on the value of a paper currency, unlike stocks, whose value rests on the profitability of a business].

"*If the investor, instead, fears price volatility, erroneously viewing it as a measure of risk, he may, ironically, end up doing some very risky things.* Recall, if you will, the pundits who six years ago [during the GFC] bemoaned falling stock prices and advised investing in "safe" Treasury bills or bank certificates of deposit. People who heeded this sermon are now earning a pittance on sums they had previously expected would finance a pleasant retirement. (The S&P 500 was then below 700; now it is about 2,100.) If not for their fear of meaningless price volatility, these investors could have assured themselves of a good income for life by simply buying a very low-cost index fund whose dividends would trend upward over the years and whose principal would grow as well (with many ups and downs, to be sure).

"Investors, of course, can, by their own behaviour, make stock ownership highly risky. And many do. Active trading, attempts to 'time' market movements, inadequate diversification, the

No issue weathering the bulls and bears when
sound long-term investments have been made.

payment of high and unnecessary fees to managers and advisors, and the use of borrowed money can destroy the decent returns that a life-long owner of equities would otherwise enjoy. Indeed, borrowed money has no place in the investor's tool kit: anything can happen anytime in markets. And no advisor, economist, or TV commentator – and definitely not Charlie [Munger, his deputy at Berkshire Hathaway] nor I – can tell you when chaos will occur. Market forecasters will fill your ear but will never fill your wallet."

Now that we have made the necessary distinction between volatility and risk, we must still face the fact that there is very real risk in the stock market. However, this risk can and must be *managed*, just like the innumerable risks that we face in just living our lives.

Develop Independence Of Thought

You must have heard the term 'herd mentality' used to death, but it is a very real part of our evolutionary nature that may have been useful in our caveman days, but in modern times places our financial future in jeopardy.

You would also probably have heard the famous Buffett dictum: "Be fearful when others are greedy, and greedy only when others are fearful."

He is speaking about contrarianism, the rejection of popular opinion. And this is a form of independence of thought, something that takes years to fully develop – especially for those of us who do not have an independent streak.

To do as Buffett said is easier said than done. At its extremes, it can be like walking into a building as everyone is fleeing; or leaving the building when an endless crowd is streaming in. It means going against our own evolutionary nature; but that ability is something that distinguishes us humans from animals, so we should believe we can do it.

So what should we do? In theory, if we apply contrarianism to its logical conclusion, we should just hold onto all our cash and wait, wait, wait until we get another full-blown meltdown like the Asian Financial Crisis of 1997 or the US subprime collapse or the Global Financial Crisis of 2008/09. Then pump all our capital into good-quality stocks that have been beaten black and blue.

But the problem is that this 'Crouching Tiger' is likely to get very sore thighs and collapse. On an emotional and mental level, this most ambitious strategy is virtually impossible to pull off. You can wait year after year as inflation causes the purchasing power of your cash to shrivel away, while this stock or that stock becomes a two-, five- or twenty-bagger.

Hence it is far more realistic to gradually put most of your investible funds in the market at very reasonable if not incredible bargain prices, but keep a moderate portion – 15 to 30 percent – in reserve, to take advantage of extraordinary opportunities. This reserve can be held in cash or high-grade bonds that are not more than twelve months from maturity (so that their price is quite stable and they can be quickly liquidated, probably without significant loss, to pursue stock opportunities).

If the market becomes very overvalued by objective measures – for instance, price to book, forward price-to-earnings ratios (PE), or PE compared to growth – then it is alright to take plenty of profit and keep up to 50 percent cash. But I would not sell everything. If you do so, you might hesitate to get back into some businesses with great long-term prospects – especially if the stock continues rising – and you might miss out on some astounding long-term growth stories.

Of course, we should not rush into the market. Patience in waiting for the right stock at the right price is still essential. But in the next paragraph, I mainly want to counter the popular notion that to find a buying opportunity, one needs to wait till the cows come home.

It is very important to stress that there are worthwhile opportunities to invest in at any time, not only in extremely bearish markets. As mentioned before, the market is not a monolith. There will always be some sectors and companies that are getting too much attention and are overvalued, and others that are neglected and undervalued, at any given time.

Let me provide two examples. In May 2016, Singapore-listed Food Empire, a multinational food and beverage maker, was trading at 26 cents, which I felt to be a tremendous bargain. A major part of its earnings came from Russia and Ukraine, where geopolitical turmoil and armed conflict had caused the currencies to crumble. But the situation was easing, and the currencies were strengthening. It was also establishing a foothold in new markets like Indochina and building up new business segments.

At the time, the *overall market* was not at crisis levels or 'bombed out' by any means. The Straits Times Index (STI) stood in the 2,700s, which was around 70 percent above its 2009 crisis low of about 1,594.87. But Food Empire, due to its own unique circumstances, was trading at crisis levels. It has since rebounded to 67 cents as of 22 Jan 2018 – a 157.7 percent capital gain in under two years.

My second example is semiconductor equipment solutions provider AEM Holdings, also listed in Singapore. In Jan 2017, the STI had already breached the 3,000 mark – not far from double its crisis lows. AEM was trading at about 63 cents. At that point, if you had done your due diligence, you would have seen the financial results for the third quarter of its Financial Year 2016 (FY16) and learned that the company's revenue had grown 53 percent to $50.6 m, while net profit had surged 213.2 percent to $3.8 m in the first nine months of the financial year. For the third quarter alone, the growth was even more impressive – 69.9 percent and 328.7 percent, respectively. In January, the full-year earnings for FY16 had not been released yet.

The company had been going through a process of restructuring and intensive R & D in the last five years to turn around a struggling business. In Jan 2017, these diligent efforts were starting to seriously bear fruit. The earnings per share (EPS) for the first nine months of FY16 alone was 8.7 cents. Even if they made zero profit for the final quarter, the stock would have been trading at only 63/8.7 = 7.2 times earnings. This would be a very reasonable valuation even for a company with steady earnings, but for a company that was seeing tremendous growth in revenue and profit, it was very cheap.

What happened after that? AEM's earnings went from strength to strength, with net profit of $21.8 m for the first nine months of Financial Year 2017, and the stock closed the year at $3.35[9]. If you had bought it at 63 cents in January, you would have made a 432 percent capital gain and an additional 7.2 percent from dividends paid – in one year!

I have a friend who made this phenomenal profit. How was it possible to do so well when buying in a market that was trading at quite normal levels and not depressed? He bought into an innovative business that was neglected by the market after years of poor earnings, and recognised its tremendous ongoing turnaround before others did.

This is independence of thought: the market was unfairly sceptical towards this business even though it had been reporting rapidly improving numbers for twenty-one months and paying dividends again. My friend thought differently and was not afraid to act on his independent, logical opinion.

Independence of thought should also extend to the way we receive 'expert opinion'. As anyone who has followed markets for a long time would know, experts often get it wrong. Even the best investors like Warren Buffett can make dreadful mistakes. And sometimes the experts (this includes stock analysts) have a hidden agenda in the opinions they espouse. How do you know that the person isn't calling a 'Buy' so that his buddy who is holding a huge position can make a killing, and then share it with him? Do not follow anyone blindly, not me, not Warren Buffett. *Do not hero worship.* Think for yourself – it's *your* money.

Recognise The Power Of Dividends

Buy low, sell high, they say. The popular notion of the stock market is that you make your profit by running in and out. But remember that a stock is *a piece of a business.* If you invested $10,000 in a friend's hardware store, surely you would expect him to share the profit with you and expect this stream of income to be a major part of your returns. It is no different from listed enterprises – if they are profitable, they should pay you dividends. "Give me my fair share," you should demand of them.

There are studies that claim that 90 percent of total returns are attributable to dividends and dividend growth, while some say it is 50 or 30 percent.[10] Much depends on the datasets and timeframes used.

But let us not obsess with academic studies, and focus more on Common Sense and practical realities. If we do that, we will realise that dividends can contribute a very substantial proportion of our returns, and that they are a great way to build up our financial health.

First we must understand two very important ratios. One is called the payout ratio, and the other, dividend yield. Payout ratio is the percentage of net profit that the company gives out to its shareholders. It can be anything from 0 to 100 percent. If it is less than 15 percent, there had better be good reasons, for instance the company has just returned to the black after a tough few years. If it is 15-25 percent, that is reasonable if the business is expanding and needs to retain a lot of profit to fund capital expenditure (land, factories, machines, new hotels, etc). Some firms pay out 50 percent or more of their earnings because they are not expanding much if at all; but some other companies give you the best of both worlds – a high payout of 50 percent or more combined with healthy growth in the business. How do they do this? They may be generating so much free cashflow that they can grow while keeping just a small portion of profit and/or have low capital expenditure (capex) requirements. A legendary example of this is See's Candy, one of the best investments made by Warren Buffett's Berkshire Hathaway. Such enterprises often make the best investments – they pay you well in terms of dividends, and with the relatively modest amounts of retained earnings they can grow the business and return you even bigger dividends in future.

Dividend yield is the ratio of the dividend per share to the price per share. For instance, if a stock is trading at $1 per share and pays 5 cents per share a year in dividend, then dividend yield is 5 percent. This is another very important ratio as it determines the rate of return you can receive for just holding the stock. It tells you how many dollars you get every year (and every month) for every hundred or thousand dollars you put into the stock.

If you can buy a decent dividend-paying stock when it is undervalued or the price is depressed, you can get an extraordinarily high dividend yield. Or sometimes the yield now might not be so attractive, but the prospect of earnings growth in coming years is strong. In such instances the yield could be a modest 4 percent today, but reach 6 percent in two years' time and 10 percent in five years.

The beauty of dividends is manifold. One is that it is passive income that augments your income from work and boosts your family's cashflow. Let's say you are just starting out, and you invest $2,000 in a stock yielding 5 percent. You get $100 dividends a year or $8.33 a month. It can buy you a meal. After you have saved more, you buy another $2,000 of that stock and $2,000 of a different stock that yields 6 percent, and your monthly dividend income grows to $26.67 – this can pay for two bags of groceries. In time to come, it may cover 20 percent of your regular household expenses, then 50 percent. When it reaches 100 percent, you will have reached at least a basic state of financial freedom. Some may say they want a passive income of 130 percent of their monthly expenses before they consider themselves financially free, as they want to have some extra money for bigger overseas holidays, children's future education at a prestigious institution like Oxford, and unforeseen expenses.

Of course, for one reason or another, not all of us will be able to attain total financial freedom. But even if you succeed partially – say, achieving dividend streams that cover 30 or 40 percent of household spending – it will still lighten your load substantially. You may have the luxury of switching to a less stressful job, working part-time, taking a few months off and so on.

Thus, planning to achieve financial independence is a most worthwhile endeavour. Even if you don't succeed completely, it is likely that you will still improve your life and that of your family, and give yourself more options and more of this precious commodity called freedom.

Seek Fellowship With Other Investors

Many believe that investing is a loner's game, and in many ways it is. The decisions we make are highly personal as they involve our own money, and we often need to be fiercely independent in mind and go against the crowd to buy a stock that is unloved by the market.

However, it can be highly enriching (in more than one sense of the word) to engage with other investors and form informal groups for discussion and sharing. You can make contacts and friends at the AGMs of listed companies, investor seminars and other events, or online at various investment forums.

I personally chair a group of more than twenty-five value investors who have been meeting once a month for several years now. We exchange views on various stocks, as well as on the general state of the market and corporate governance issues. We speak freely and frankly, and it is good to test your views against other sharp minds and experienced hands. In doing this you will discover your blind spots, and develop a deeper understanding. You can also pool the information unearthed by the various members' research, which will give you access to a much larger body of data and investment ideas than you would have on your own.

Work out how small or large a group you want to put together. A word of advice: be selective about whom you make a permanent member of a group. If you bring in someone whose approach or personality is incompatible with the group, it can upset the chemistry. One solution is to invite someone as a guest for a few sessions first before you make them a permanent member.

Plan And Invest For The Long Term

Financial literacy and its acquisition is a life-long journey. Financial plans and investments are for the long term and the best rewards come when you are able to hold your investments through major downturns and reap the benefits when good times roll again.

You have to be the master of your investments and not their slave. By that I mean you must be able or have the means to make a stock or bond or property purchase when the opportunity arises; especially when they offer very good value. At the same time, you should not be forced to make a sale because your cashflow has dried up and the bank is chasing you for some repayments or the family needs cash for daily expenses. The best gains in investments are derived when you have the choice of when to sell. This should be when you assess the investment to be fully valued or overpriced.

You have to start on the journey as early as possible with the right attitude and basics in place. You will get better as you read and practise what you learn in a disciplined way, with long-term objectives in mind. I am sure you can do it!

1 Venture Corporation was listed on the Singapore bourse in 1992 at 40 cents. On 11 Jan 2018, it closed at $22.40. There was a 1-for-2 rights issue and a 1-for-1 bonus issue in 1996. Including all dividends paid, Venture has returned 18,559 percent since listing.

2 Hsin-hun made this remark in an illuminating interview with the Financially Free Now blog. You can read it at https://financiallyfreenow.wordpress.com/2012/09/15/coffee-with-ffn-and-wan/

3 "99% of actively managed US equity funds underperform", Chris Newland and Madison Marriage, *Financial Times*, 24 Oct 2016 https://www.ft.com/content/e139d940-977d-11e6-a1dc-bdf38d484582

4 Jason Zweig, in his commentary to *The Intelligent Investor* (Revised Edition), Benjamin Graham, 1973. New material by Jason Zweig, 2003. PerfectBound (publisher).

5 "A simple no-fuss approach to investing in stocks", Aaron Low, *The Straits Times*, 21 Aug 2016 http://www.straitstimes.com/business/a-simple-no-fuss-approach-to-investing-in-stocks

6 "Dollar cost averaging just means taking risk later", Vanguard Research, 2012 https://personal.vanguard.com/pdf/s315.pdf

7 "Invest now or temporarily hold your cash?", Vanguard Research, 2016 https://personal.vanguard.com/pdf/ISGDCA.pdf

8 *Concentrated Investing: Strategies of the World's Greatest Concentrated Value Investors*, Allen C. Benello, Michael van Biema, Tobias E. Carlisle, Published by Wiley, 2016

9 AEM Holdings awarded shareholders a 3-for-1 bonus issue in May 2018, meaning that you would receive three new shares for every one that you had. Thus if you wish to compare the share price before and after May 2018, you need to multiply the later share price by four as the total number of shares in issue had increased fourfold. . Do note also that when you look up stock charts on Google and other sources, the historical prices may also have been adjusted for the bonus issue. For instance, as of 8 Jul 2018, Google's chart says that the price in Jan 2017 was 15-16c when at the time, it was actually trading four times higher.

10 "Dividends' True Contribution to Total Return May Surprise You", Chuck Carnevale, Yahoo Finance, 25 Mar 2016, https://finance.yahoo.com/news/dividends-true-contribution-total-return-204309083.html

CHAPTER 6

PROPERTY AND REITS

A book on financial planning and investment for the long term cannot possibly be complete without a section or chapter on property and its equity counterpart, REITs or Real Estate Investment Trusts. Investment in property or real estate is as old as Singapore while the concept of REITs has taken on great popularity and relevance in the last twenty years or so.

PROPERTY VERSUS STOCKS: WHICH SHOULD I FOCUS MY INVESTMENTS ON?

There really is no one right answer for this. The choice varies according to each individual's situation, behavioural traits and preferences. Numerous investors have built their financial freedom in either real estate or stocks, or a varying mix of both.

What's important is to understand the differences between the two asset classes. When you invest directly in real estate – land and/or bricks and mortar – you get a very tangible, physical asset (provided you actually see and touch it, and don't just buy some building far away that your agent shows you a picture of!). The solidity of the asset is a source of assurance, provided the supply-demand dynamics are in its favour – for instance, it can easily attract tenants instead of sitting empty collecting cobwebs for years. A piece of real estate is in your hands and tangible, rather than a share of common stock in a company which is a rather more abstract asset and not in your control. With your own piece of real estate, you don't need to worry about someone else controlling it and manipulating its accounts.

However, for property to be a viable option, it is crucial that incomes must be rising on average and in a steady pattern on the back of an improving economy. Security and political stability is a given. Then only will the property market stay on a long-term uptrend and reward owners with returns that are far above the inflation rate. These factors have all been at play in Singapore over the past fifty years or so, and property owners have done well. Most Singaporeans live in Housing and Development Board or HDB apartments and their family wealth is significantly tied to the value of their homes.

For the government, too, the ever-rising values of land have been a major boon in building up the country's reserves. The proceeds of land sales over the years have gone straight to the reserves and these have been invested in foreign assets to provide a cushion for the future, should the country face hard times. Singapore's operational national budgets have also taken prudent approaches over the years and the surpluses from these have also found their way into foreign investments via the Government of Singapore Investment Corporation (GIC or GIC Private Limited) or Temasek Holdings. These sovereign funds invest in both property (commercial and industrial) and companies (their shares and bonds).

One major disadvantage of property though is its very chunky nature, financially speaking. It is rare to find an apartment, office or factory space that won't cost a middle-income earner many years of his savings. If he commits to a direct property purchase, chances are that he will have very little free cashflow left to invest in anything else for years or even decades. Diversification of investment would be very difficult, particularly for middle- and lower-income investors. Another issue is that most people will need to take up a sizeable debt to finance this investment, meaning that you have to pay a quite princely sum in interest over the span of the loan, typically about twenty years. If you can collect enough rental and interest rates stay manageable, then all is fine. But if one or both of these factors turn against you, things can become quite dire, as mentioned earlier. Of course, debt is a double-edged sword and can work in your favour as well. If you select a good property and buy at the right price, the debt will multiply your profits many times. Leverage can work powerfully for or against you – so pull that lever wisely!

Unlike real estate, stocks allow investments in small- to medium-sized bites and without taking on debt. It is far more feasible for the average person to have a diversified basket of stocks (say eight to thirty) than a diversified basket of properties. This is excellent for risk management.

This is why this book focuses primarily on stocks as most readers will be middle- or lower-income, and it is my position that stocks make a more suitable investment mainstay for these groups.

KNOW YOUR REAL ESTATE INVESTMENT TRUSTS

But if, as a middle- or lower-income earner, you have a strong desire to be vested in physical property without most of the pitfalls mentioned above, there is a wonderful place where property and stocks converge – and that is, *Real Estate Investment Trusts or REITs*. These are professionally managed investment funds that raise capital from shareholders and use it to acquire properties. The funds then manage those properties, find tenants and pay what is usually a generous dividend to shareholders after deducting costs.

Thus REITs are a good way for the man or woman in the street to gain access to property investments on a manageable scale. You can buy into properties, indirectly, with just a few hundred dollars at a time, without incurring debt.

I recall vividly how our capital markets team at DBS was conceptualising and working on documentation in respect of the first big local REIT to be floated on SGX or the Singapore Exchange. That was in the years 1999 and 2000. The REIT involved was CapitaLand Mall Trust (CMT) which remains today one of the most popular and successful REITs listed on the SGX.

At that time, however, there were doubts among investors as to whether it made sense to invest in a trust that was heavy on assets that had been revalued and which offered little discount to its underlying Net Asset Value or NAV. The trust was also relatively heavy on borrowings, with its debt-to-equity ratio at about 50 percent. Gearing, or borrowings against total assets, stood at about 33 percent.

The main attraction was that the REIT, named CMT in short, promised to pay at least 90 percent of its net income after all expenses. Why did it plan to be so generous in its dividend payouts? The government had made it a condition that REITs which paid out 90 percent of their net income would enjoy tax concessions. The dividends would be tax-free in the hands of individual shareholders (REIT shareholders are typically called unit holders in Singapore).

The government's motive was to promote Singapore as a centre for REITs. This would add to the depth of the property and equity markets, it was considered. DBS, which is substantially owned by Temasek Holdings, was tasked with floating the first REIT.

However, there were and still are other options for local investors wanting to invest in property through the equity or stock market. Well-established developers like Singapore Land and CapitaLand, even in the year 2000, offered the opportunity to buy quality property assets at a good discount to underlying net asset value. They paid dividends regularly and even if their yields were not as attractive as that proposed by CMT, the discounts to net asset values provided good defensive cushions. I, too, was not convinced at that time that it made sense to buy CMT at a dollar and enjoy a 6 percent yield but without downside protection on capital value. Singapore Land, with a 4 percent yield and 30 percent discount to NAV made more sense.

The floatation of CMT was a success, but not a great one. Due to the size of the float and the newness of the REIT idea, I recall it traded close to offer price for some time. It was only much later that the price moved gradually upwards as the REIT continued to pay regular dividends every three months and as the value of the underlying shopping malls appreciated. CMT also showed that its managers were adept at maximising returns on its assets through upgrading and expansion works on its portfolio of properties.

As returns improved, the net income also rose steadily through the years. CMT made acquisitions of new malls from its parent company, CapitaLand. It has also bought assets from third parties, where the managers considered that the assets would yield sufficient returns to enhance *dividend per unit* or *DPU* for existing holders.

As the DPU crept up over the years, so did the value of the underlying units. CMT units generally trade above $2 nowadays and the yield hovers between 4.5 percent and 5.5 percent, depending on the general market. The NAV is just below the $2 mark. Market capitalisation of CMT is a whopping $7.4 b as I write.

Investors in CMT since its IPO have done very well overall. On their original $1 per unit, they would have enjoyed a gradual increase in DPU from about 6 cents to the current 11 cents or so. The unit price of the trust has more than doubled, even after adjustment for intervening placements of units to raise fresh funds for expansion. But the stock has languished in the last three years due to various factors, including competition from online retailers and the downside pressure on rentals of shops in its portfolio of malls.

Further, it has not been a straight, upward sloping line for net income, dividends and net asset values and stock prices. There were difficult periods between 2004 and 2006 and also during the US Financial Crisis in 2008 and 2009. These were slow periods in the Singapore economy and the stock market traded at depressed values. However, CMT units recovered their values as consumer sentiments improved, showing the resilience of the trust and its strategy.

The REIT sector in Singapore is now a large one, with very healthy growth shown in many trusts operating across a wide swathe of property segments and geographies. SGX now features a good selection of not only Retail REITs like CMT, but investors are also spoilt for choice in the Commercial, Industrial/

Logistics and Hospitality sectors. Analysts cover all the sectors and provide information on asset values, gearing and DPU.

My sense is that many Singapore investors, especially the older ones, have a very heavy commitment in REITs. Over the years, they have learnt that REITs are reliable generators of dividends which are paid quarterly in many cases. Where certain REITs have over-expanded and been caught in tight cash situations during downturns, they have usually been rescued or bought out by stronger entities keen to enter the sector. But when they are rescued or bought out, it may not be on terms that are favourable to existing unit holders. By and large, the experience in REITs has been good for Singapore-based investors over the past eighteen years. The Monetary Authority of Singapore keeps a close eye on the sector in terms of its governance and debt levels. This has helped to prevent scandals that we have seen in other sectors of SGX.

Notably, the hype over mainland Chinese companies listing on SGX has all but totally fizzled out. S-chips, as they are known, have been involved in one scandal after another, so much so that investors have written off their substantial losses and given up on them. Even well-run S-chips with growing profits and market presence are being neglected due to the missing trust factor.

In contrast, the investor following for REITs has been growing. It is seen as a relatively safe sector and the annual general meetings of many REITs are packed with retirees happy with their steady incomes from this sector. Many are looking to increase their investments and, consequently, income flows.

However, it would be wise to pause and reconsider. For myself and many value investors, REITs are not the panacea to all investment woes. They are not necessarily the only way to earn a steady passive income with little overall risk.

There are risks inherent in REITs which have not shown themselves much in recent years. Hence the investor complacency.

One must go back to basic concepts about property investment and risks inherent in order to understand REITs. It is said that fire is a good servant and a bad master. The same applies to investment in property. You must be in control of your investment and not have it the other way around. Buy as much property as you can comfortably hold if you have the sustainable means to service the loans and mortgages.

Remember the variables can change. For example, interest rates can rise unexpectedly, and unless you have invested with a margin of safety, you could be caught servicing expensive mortgages at relatively high interest rates. That will affect the cashflow you need for other purposes. Another variable that can change without warning is the rental you derive from your investment property. In a glut situation, rentals will drop and your income flow will be slower than expected. In the worst case, you might not even be able to find a tenant for long periods. Go on the Internet and search 'ghost malls', for instance, and you will get an idea of how desolate your property can become if you read the market and supply-demand dynamics wrongly.

If *both* variables come into play at the same time, then you will really be caught on the wrong foot. The mortgages will cost more while rental income dwindles or disappears. Your cashflow from the investment could be negative, requiring you to dig into reserves to cover the deficit and keep your lenders at bay. If you are not able to service the loans, there may be pressure to sell the property.

Your woes may not end there. In an environment of rising interest rates and falling rentals, it is very likely that capital values will also go down. This is what happened during various property downcycles in Singapore and elsewhere. Like fire, the property will then be controlling you. You will need to get out of the situation to save yourself but that could mean selling at a loss. In a fire-sale, the value derived may not even be sufficient to pay off the outstanding mortgage.

At the end of it, you could be left standing without the investment property and shrunken cash reserves intended for your retirement. So, don't rush into investment property during the good times without doing proper projections of cashflow and possible negative turns in the interest rate and rental cycles.

Likewise, for REITs. These property trusts usually do well when the sun is shining, when the economy is growing and rentals are steadily rising due to increasing demand – be it for retail shops, offices, hotel rooms and industrial space or warehouses. In the early years of the economic upswing, interest rates usually remain benign.

So REITs enjoy the sweet spot – low cost of borrowings, rising rentals and appreciating capital values of their assets. Some of them may go on acquisition sprees and buy assets at revalued, inflated prices so as to boost growth in their portfolios and enjoy higher management fees. The acquisitions are not necessarily in the interests of unit holders who may have to pay out new cash to pick up rights issues[1] and fund the purchases. The managers of the REITs may also need to borrow more against the underlying assets.

Potential Pitfalls Of REIT Investments

All could be well for a couple of years but if or when the cycle takes a downturn, with a glut in property on the market, higher interest rates and lower incomes on property portfolios, then the expansionists will have cause for worry.

The REITs involved will come under pressure. Their incomes will go down due to declining rentals while cost of borrowings is on the uptrend. They could attempt to sell part of their portfolio to raise cash but the market will be against them. It may be a buyers' market then, meaning the buyers call the shots and not the sellers. So, such REITs will have few options but to make fresh cash calls from investors (capital raising through rights issues and preferential offers).

Rights issues can be quite common among REITs in a depressed property market as the managers attempt to reduce borrowings and stay cashflow positive. Unit holders will be asked to bail them out with fresh cash. So part or even all of the cash these holders have received in dividends is 'returned' to the REITs. In some cases, unit holders may have to put in more than what they have earned from the REITs over their entire investment. Of course one can sell off her new shares or units to recoup her cash or even make a profit, but this can only be done if and when the price is right.

The sad part is that rights issues are often made in poor economic times, which means they affect the cash reserves of investors at the worst possible time. To exacerbate matters, dividends are sometimes cut following the rights issues, which then affects recurrent passive income of REIT investors.

My purpose in explaining the risks inherent in property and REIT investment is to sound a warning that REITs are not the panacea to the cashflow problems of older investors. Dividend yield is not everything. Do consider the downside risk in capital values should your REITs be caught unawares in an economic or financial downturn, local or global.

Most REITs have sizeable borrowings and keep little cash. A large proportion of their cash is paid out to investors while the going is good. Few REITs trade at a significant discount to their underlying asset values as their high dividend payouts attract investors. But the happy equation can go completely off-balance when negative factors prevail.

Even in good times, a rights issue or preferential offer can be called to help finance a property acquisition. If you observe the REIT market for years, it becomes quite clear that some REITs are far more fond of making such cash calls than others. They do it every three years or so, while others never do it – instead raising capital through increasing bank loans or placing out new shares to third parties. Thus if you prefer to avoid being asked to pump in fresh capital, you might want to lean towards those REITs in the latter category.

A brief note on the difference between rights issues and preferential offers[2]. Rights issues are usually renounceable, meaning that if you do not wish to pay out the money to subscribe to your rights (and convert them into shares or units), you can sell them on the market during a specified period and get some compensation for the dilution of your shareholding – although you will most likely have to sell them at a discount to fair value as buyers would not be interested in your rights otherwise. However, preferential offers are not renounceable. If you do not take up your entitlement, there will be no compensation for the dilution you suffer (as new shares or units are issued, your percentage stake in the REIT diminishes if you do not take up these new shares and others do).

The frequency of these cash calls (i.e. rights issues and preferential offers) is partly dependent on how active a REIT is in acquiring real estate. Be aware that some REITs do this more often than others; in some cases it is because they have a parent company that is a large developer with an extensive pipeline of buildings for its REIT to buy. While the transactions are supposed to be conducted "at arm's length", one has to scrutinise the details to decide whether they are on terms that are fair or favourable to the REIT unit holder.

It should be stressed that cash calls are not necessarily a bad thing. Sometimes they are done from a position of strength, and with unit holders' interests in mind. For instance, the REIT may be picking up a building with outstanding redevelopment potential at a good price. After you pony up the money, you might see the building produce an excellent return over the years and give you a great return on your additional capital, which you can realise by selling off the new shares you purchased via the rights issue.

Rights issues and preferential offers also provide another avenue of opportunity for the disciplined investor: the chance to pick up some "excess rights" or "excess shares". These are rights units or shares that other unit holders were entitled to but were unwilling or unable (or forgot) to subscribe to. You can apply for this "excess" (in Singapore, you currently can do so via ATM or a paper form) and if you are lucky, the REIT will allocate some to you. It is a sure-win in most cases as rights and preferential offer shares are almost invariably priced at a substantial discount to market price. But of course you need capital to subscribe not only for your entitlement, but some "excess" as well. Unit holders who are disciplined about maintaining a portion of investible assets in cash have a big advantage in this regard.

This leads me to my next point. If you hold REITs in your portfolio, it would be wise to set aside some cash to meet any cash calls. You will want to have enough cash to take up your entitlement, and ideally subscribe for some excess rights/ shares as well. How much cash to set aside depends on how much REITs you hold and also the propensity of your REITs to make cash calls. The strong REITs rarely issue more than one rights share for every five or six existing, and it is at a significant discount. So you should have no problem taking up your entitlement if you put aside a sum of cash equal to 15-20 percent of the market value of your holdings in that REIT.

But in the case of weak REITs (notably those without a strong parent company or sponsor), they may do massive fund-raising exercises of one or even two or three rights shares for every one existing! What we learned in the 2008-2009 Global Financial Crisis is that REITs without a strong parent or sponsor can be caught in a quagmire when bank credit freezes up and they are unable to refinance their maturing loans. In such cases, they need to raise a massive amount of capital and the demands on your finances could be severe. It is probably best to avoid such weaker entities.

When, however, a REIT has a strong parent or sponsor (for instance, CapitaLand Commercial Trust is backed by property giant CapitaLand), banks are much more willing to extend loans to them especially in tough times. And even if the banks were to refuse to lend, the REIT's parent can often provide the financing.

So, my advice is that it is fine to invest in REITs, but do pick and choose which REITs you want to put your faith in.

They should be well-governed with the aspirations of the REIT managers aligned with those of the unit holders. Examine their track records to see how they have grown DPU over the years while maintaining borrowings and costs at sensible levels.

Currently, Singapore REITs (S-REITs) are subjected to a gearing (defined in this case as total debt divided by total assets) limit of 45 percent. As of 11 June 2018, the average gearing for S-REITs varied from 32.7 percent for retail REITs (those owning shopping malls) to 37.1 percent for office REITs[3]. Compare the gearing level of a particular REIT with that of its peers and consider whether it is prudent vis-a-vis its earnings stability. Some REITs have more stable and resilient earnings than others. For instance, one that owns suburban malls selling daily necessities in high-density housing estates is likely to have a more recession-proof business than another that owns malls selling Versace and Bulgari on a posh downtown shopping street. A REIT whose properties are located in areas where there is limited competition or potential competition (for instance, due to a lack of land for further developments) is likely to be more stable than one where there is plenty.

In my opinion, it would be sensible to ensure that your investment in REITs does not make up too large a portion of your overall portfolio of value stocks that have growth potential and pay decent dividends. Percentages can vary, but for me, as an illustration, REITs do not constitute more than 20 per cent of my overall portfolio by value. I also do not own any physical property other than the family home jointly owned with my spouse. If, however, you wish to build a portfolio that contains more than 50 percent in REITs, do make sure that you have sufficient diversification in terms of the number of REITs, the sponsors behind them, the types of properties they hold (for instance retail, industrial and hospitality) and the geographies in which their assets are located (at least three different countries); and that you set aside sufficient cash (commensurate to the value of your REIT holdings) to get a good deal for yourself during cash calls.

PHYSICAL PROPERTY

If, however, you are keener on physical property and like the idea of being a landlord, then do by all means consider investing in property other than your home. Singapore has a well-established property market which offers opportunities to own residential, commercial and even industrial property. You could even enter the hospitality industry by purchasing a row of shophouses which lend themselves to restoration and conversion to a boutique hotel charging premium room rates.

I know of friends who have made a small fortune investing in numerous properties over the decades. Most of them, however, come from well-to-do families who already have strong financial bases made up of family-owned cash-generating businesses with some land or property asset underlying them.

The first, pioneer and entrepreneurial generation built up the business from scratch, after landing in Singapore from China or India or elsewhere. As the founders aged, the children took over and as their businesses evolved, this second, usually more-educated, generation moved to either upgrade the core business or develop the underlying land and property assets.

Where their properties were not wholly acquired by the government for development needs, the families were able to build up significant portfolios of properties. Given Singapore's steady economic growth over the last fifty years or so, incomes have also been on the rise and these, in turn, have facilitated the rise in the values of properties.

Today, the wealthiest individuals and families in Singapore have their foundation in property. There are some who have done well in other industries, but the majority of Singapore's billionaires made their fortunes in property. Names that come to mind include the families of Ng Teng Fong, Khoo Teck Puat, Kwek Leng Beng, Robert Kuok, Kwees of Pontiac Land and the brothers of the Royal group.

There are many others of notable financial clout who built their wealth on the long-term rising values of property in Singapore. One could go further to say that most Singaporeans have their wealth tied to their property assets, be it just a single landed property or a small HDB apartment. The government has helped to ensure that steady economic growth, overall security and an expanding population underpin a very healthy property market.

The Ups And Downs Of The Property Market

But there have been ups and downs for the property market even in land-scarce Singapore. It has not been a straight line up and we have seen sharp reversals in 1973/74 (OPEC and the crude oil supply crisis), 1985/86 (economic recession), 1997/98 (Asian Financial Crisis) and 2008/09 (the US financial crisis).

This upcycle started in 2006 and it is still going strong after twelve years, with only a small reversal between 2008 and 2009. Thereafter, despite the government's efforts to cool the market, the undertone has been firm. A long period of low interest rates and easy credit have helped the market remain on the uptrend, as investors look for assets in which to park their surplus funds.

In Singapore, as in many cities around the world, property has been the favourite asset in the last ten years at least.

So, is it a good time, all things considered, to buy a property right now? Is the uptrend going to persist so much so that we see regular appreciation of capital values in the residential, commercial and industrial sectors? I would be cautious at this stage.

My sense is that the upcycle has gone on for too long and values have been inflated to a level that they may not be sustainable. For example, in the private residential property market, Singapore is seeing a frenzy of en-bloc sales. Entire condominiums of good, liveable condition are being bought over by developers at sky-high prices. The conventional logic is that developers are starved of land bank and the government sales of land are drawing stiff competition and high prices. So it is 'cheaper' for developers to take the route of buying out entire condominiums and rebuilding on the land.

The government, on its part, allows higher plot ratios for the rebuilt condominiums if the developers are prepared to pay a premium or development cost. The leases on the land can also be topped up to 99 years. This means it is like a new project with land purchased from the government.

The developers make their money through more intensive development of the land, with taller buildings and more, but smaller, units. They appear more affordable to young, aspiring families upgrading from HDB or public housing apartments even though the small apartments are at relatively high prices in per sq ft terms.

So far, it has been so good and this has worked. But I think the sweet music will stop at some stage when buyers realise

"Do you have anything that matches our $200k budget?"

"We sold it in 1993."

the upside in values is limited and the units are too small for growing families.

If interest rates keep rising, as they appear to be set to do for the next couple of years, then the property market could see a new top followed by a stepped downturn that could last some years. No one can say how deep the downturn will be but it would be wrong to think that the Singapore property market is incapable of suffering big falls. We saw what happened in 1997/98 when values were almost halved for most residential properties.

My advice would be to carefully manage exposure to physical property at this stage. If you own a portfolio of properties, sell a few, reduce your debt level and keep some cash in reserve. The time will come when your strong financial situation will be an asset. Likewise, for young couples, it will make sense to defer any purchase until the market has corrected itself significantly. Let the current euphoria run out of steam and wait for a more sober period to emerge. You will know it when it comes. People will not be talking about property at social gatherings or if they do, they will lament the poor state of the market.

In biding your time, do consider renting a property if you really need a home. Rental yields are low and so it is a good market for those wanting to have a roof over their heads. Make a commitment for two years and see what happens. Do not be too worried about runaway home prices; bear in mind that they can and will reverse direction in due course.

Personally, I refused to upgrade our home during the persistent residential property uptrend from 1990 to 1996. We were then staying in an HUDC[4] maisonette in Bedok Reservoir Road. The newspapers were full of stories about how people could be left behind if they did not purchase a roof over their heads or upgrade quickly.

Our HUDC apartment was then worth more than $700,000 in 1996, a record price in those days. But by late 1998, the price had fallen to only $400,000, no thanks to the various problems linked to the Asian Financial Crisis. Fortunately for us, we stuck to our guns through the uptrend and built up our cash and CPF reserves. Then, in late 1998, at the height of the financial crisis, we made a decisive move to look for a private property.

After an exhaustive search involving the whole family visiting various properties over at least six weekends, we landed ourselves our present home. It is a semi-detached house in the Tanjong Katong Estate which is bounded by Mountbatten Road, Tanjong Katong Road and Old Airport Road and the Geylang River. We were able to secure the freehold property for $1.25 m where the previous owner was not willing to let it go for even $2.7 m in 1996.

So, it seems that patience does pay. The property sits on 3,666 sq ft of land and faces the East Coast Park in a south-easterly direction. It has five en-suite rooms as well as a storeroom and a prayer room. The living room, kitchen and attic are all very spacious and airy. The house also features an upper and lower garden with the living room elevated from the road level. For us, it is an ideal home in the right location and with the right orientation. It is in a quiet neighbourhood that is not far from the city. Just a five-minute walk away is the thriving Tanjong Katong neighbourhood with its food and other service outlets. Also a few minutes away is the beautiful Geylang River and its connectors to the Kallang River and the Sports Hub.

The area is serviced by two MRT stations, Paya Lebar and Dakota, and also two highways: East Coast Parkway and the Pan Island Expressway.

We borrowed about $750,000 to buy the property, using $500,000 accumulated in my CPF to cover the balance. Then we spent $250,000 in 1999 to repair the apron of the house, build a new attic and an elevated porch linked to the living room. That sum also covered other improvements and the furniture and electrical items. The house is now worth over $5 million.

A carefully worked-out strategy to investment in physical property and REITs can provide good returns in the long term. I hope this chapter has been useful in clarifying your own thoughts on this large and important sector in Singapore.

The bottom line that emerges is that you should never allow yourself to be so heavily involved that you become a slave to real estate. Make sure you remain the master of your property and REIT investments at all times!

---

1 A rights issue is an issue of new shares offered at a special price by a company to its existing shareholders in proportion to their holding of old shares.

2 Please note that the way these terms are used and defined may vary from country to country. I have used terminology according to Singapore norms.

3 "Weekly S-REITs Tracker", OCBC Investment Research, 11 Jun 2018.

4 HUDC stands for Housing and Urban Development Company. HUDC apartments were built in the 1970s and 1980s by the Housing and Development Board (HDB) as a higher-quality public housing option for middle-income citizen families. HDB phased them out in 1987 as demand declined. HUDC developments were allowed to privatise, and most if not all have done so.

CHAPTER 7

BUY GROWTH STOCKS IN CRISIS (GSIC)

There is a tide in the affairs of men, which
taken at the flood, leads on to fortune.
Omitted, all the voyage of their life is bound in
shallows and in miseries. On such a full sea are
we now afloat. And we must take the current
when it serves, or lose our ventures.
— William Shakespeare

In Chapter 5, I said that there are good buying opportunities in the stock market at any given time, no matter how bullish or bearish the general conditions. In any kind of market, there are always some companies and stocks that are in vogue and probably overvalued, and others which are the opposite. Hence I would advise you not to be overly obsessed with general conditions.

However, it is also undeniable that *crisis* is a significant word and element in any investor's career. Crises can be classified into (a) general market crises and (b) crises that affect individual stocks and companies. I shall address each of these in turn.

GENERAL MARKET CRISES

While there are undervalued stocks and buying opportunities in any market, it is also true that they are far more abundant in a bear market, especially one that has been struck by a general market crisis.

These events are triggered by some form of trauma in the world, and it then inflicts trauma on financial markets. Those who have suffered heavy losses in such events often bear deep mental scars.

We've seen the OPEC oil crisis and heard Lee Kuan Yew's "bubble must burst" speech in 1973; then we had the Pan Electric crisis in 1983; the Asian Financial Crisis in 1997/98 and the bursting of the dotcom bubble in 2000/2001 as well as the SARS period in 2003/4. Most recently we witnessed the US-triggered Global Financial Crisis in 2008/9.

These are emotive events which we often associate with much weeping and gnashing of teeth. But let us untangle our emotions from our thoughts and our logic, and see these events objectively for what they are. The Chinese expression for 'crisis' puts it well: *wei ji.* The first character means 'danger'; the second, 'opportunity'. And that is exactly what a crisis is, whether in life or in stocks.

Therefore market crises present the kind of opportunities that a value investor will only see a few times in his or her lifetime. Fear, often on the level of hysteria, takes over and investors and speculators alike sell indiscriminately. Many babies are thrown out with the bathwater. Good and bad stocks are all beaten down to unbelievable levels. Everyone wants to exit at the same time, making it a buyers' market. This is when one has to be brave and buy your favourite growth stocks at fire sale prices.

Figure 7.1 Times of crisis = Big opportunities
Source: DBS Bank and SGX

Anatomy of the Stock Market

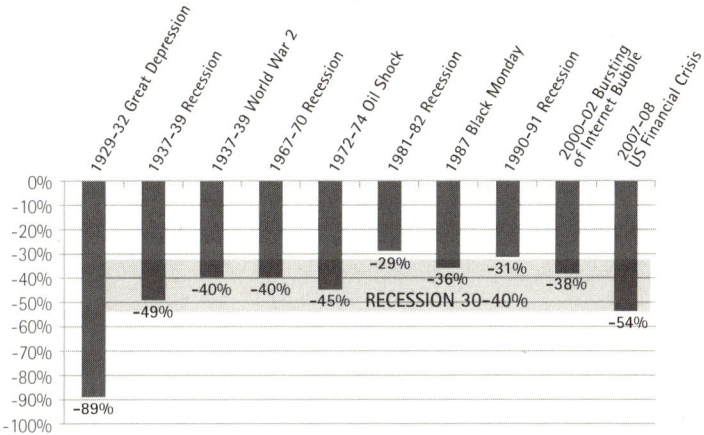

The table below highlights eight stocks listed in Singapore and how much you would have made if you had had the composure, awareness and boldness to buy in 2009.

Figure 7.2 Returns on eight Singapore listed stocks bought in 2009

Stock (Bloomberg Ticker)	Price on Feb 13, 2009 (unless other date is specified)	Price on Feb 2, 2018	Total return (after factoring in dividends and corporate actions such as rights and bonus issues)
Venture Corp (VMS:SP)	$4.05	$23.57	596%
Frasers Centrepoint Trust (FCT:SP)	$0.62	$2.23	404%
DBS Group Holdings (DBS:SP)	$6.90 (6 Mar 2009)	$26.68	360%
Kingsmen Creatives (KMEN:SP)	$0.31 (20 Feb 2009)	$0.64	205%
Raffles Medical (RFMD:SP)[1]	$0.22	$1.09	454%
Hi-P (HIP:SP)	$0.33	$1.98	610%
CDL Hospitality Trusts	$0.40 (13 Mar 2009)	$1.73	612%[2]
United Overseas Land (UOL:SP)	$1.96 (6 Feb 2009)	$9.04	422%

Crashes like this are when you have to be brave and take your positions in stocks trading at unwarranted low prices. However, you must only select the stocks of good, well-run businesses with strong balance sheets; and companies whose business models are still intact and prospects remain fair, notwithstanding the crises. This is to ensure that the company does not go belly up during the crisis, rendering your shares worthless.

In times of market panic, the valuations are so low that your cash reserves can go a long way in accumulating quality stocks. Prices could go even lower, but you have to stay the course. Be patient and let the market stabilise and then correct upwards. This could take months or even years, but it has to happen, short of a cataclysmic event happening – like a nuclear war that will set the world back for decades.

Many fear to dip their toes into the market during a crash because of the eternal question: "What if it goes lower?" At this juncture it would be useful to consider the words of Baron Rothschild: *"I will tell you my secret if you wish. It is this: I never buy at the bottom and I always sell too soon."*

This quote may confuse many a new investor, but we should all reflect on it. My interpretation is that Baron Rothschild is telling us that we cannot predict the exact movements of the market with perfect accuracy, and therefore it is silly and futile to try to catch the absolute bottom (to buy) and the absolute top (to sell). In any case one does not need to achieve anywhere close to such perfect timing to reap excellent profits.

Look at the chart of Raffles Medical Group (RMG), a leading healthcare provider in Singapore.

Figure 7.3 Uptrend on the back of steady growth
Source: Google Finance and Yahoo Finance

Raffles Medical Group Ltd.[3]
SGX: BSL – 5 Feb, 5:04 PM GMT+8

1.11 SGD ↑0.02 (1.83%)

1 day	5 day	1 month	3 month	1 year	5 year	**max**

0.18 Nov 14, 2008

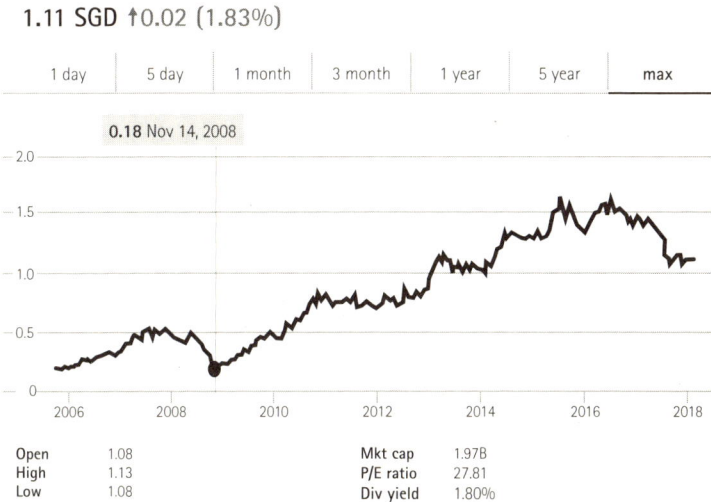

Open	1.08	Mkt cap	1.97B
High	1.13	P/E ratio	27.81
Low	1.08	Div yield	1.80%

The absolute bottom was 18 cents on 14 Nov, 2008. Suppose you had waited for the market to show significant recovery before you found the courage to go in, and you picked up some shares more than 3 months later – on 27 Feb, 2009 at 25 cents. Or worse, you were even more hesitant and waited *another 3 months and a few days more* – and finally bought into RMG on 5 June, 2009 at 35 cents. By Christmas Eve you would have been smiling – the stock had continued its steady upward climb to 48 cents. Fast forward eight years or so – and your smile would have widened even more as RMG was going for $1.11 a pop on 5 Feb, 2018. To top it off, you would have collected a sizeable amount of dividends in these eight to nine years.

Suppose you had gone in a bit early, on 5 Sep, 2008 at 34 cents. You would have had to watch as the shares dived by almost half to 18 cents on 14 Nov. But if you had stuck to your assessment of the *intrinsic value* of the stock and believed that Mr Market was just having one of his transient bouts of depression, you would have kept your cool and held on to your stock in the logical faith that sanity would return to the market in good time.

If you had sold the stock "too soon" on 2 Apr 2015 at $1.30, this time missing the top of $1.65 on 24 Jul 2015 by a considerable margin, you would still have done very well no matter which of the above-mentioned entry points you had taken. You would have grown your money by 4–6 times after counting dividends.

I trust you now understand what Baron Rothschild meant by "I never buy at the bottom, and I always sell too soon". Try your best to buy when Mr Market is going into an emotional downtrend, and sell when he is going into an emotional uptrend – but don't worry if your timing is not perfect. It's fine as long as he is giving you a fundamentally good deal.

Successful investors are not gods who know where the exact bottom or top of the market is; they just try to time their move as best they can, and most of their money is made in the middle of trends.

In each of the black swan events mentioned above, the markets bounced back smartly in a couple of years or sooner. The gains for those who went in and stood their ground were nothing short of spectacular. Stocks can double, triple or more during the broad-based recovery that follows a sharp market downturn.

STOCK-SPECIFIC CRISES

At times a crisis afflicts not the entire market, but a particular company or stock. There could be some bad news that has shaken the market's confidence in that company – a shock loss for the latest quarter, an anonymous report making serious allegations against the company, a massive write-off due to customer receivables gone sour.

The share price will usually take a big hit, and it is in times like these that a value investor will take a close look, calmly and rationally assess the bad news, and make as objective a judgement as possible on whether Mr Market has overreacted to the bad news. Being an emotional creature, he sometimes will. If he does, that presents an opportunity for the astute investor.

A good example was what happened to Singapore-listed (Hong Kong-headquartered) Valuetronics. A contract manufacturer, it has two broad lines of business: Consumer Electronics (CE) and Industrial and Commercial Electronics (ICE). In 2014, its price plummeted from 50 cents to 30 cents after it reported an 11.4 percent decline in revenue for its CE segment in the first quarter of financial year 2015 (Valuetronics' financial year or FY ends in March; therefore the quarter ending on 30 June 2014 is its first quarter for FY2015). Valuetronics was manufacturing LED lightbulbs for an MNC, which had been hit by much cheaper Chinese competition and needed to cut prices to compete. To make things worse, Valuetronics was also hit by an extremely bearish analyst report that argued that its CE segment was worth zero, and its ICE segment, only 4.4 times earnings. The analyst called a 'Sell' with a target price of 25 cents[4].

So the stock was torpedoed. But any sensible investor who maintained a calm, rational objectivity at the time would have been able to see that both the market and analyst had been far too negative in their perception of the stock. In the first quarter of FY2015 (1Q15), Valuetronics' overall results had actually been decent. Revenue had grown 2.5 percent to HK$626.6 m, and net profit by 1.8 percent to HK$33.9 m. Both top and bottom lines were rising, albeit slowly, and overall profit margins largely maintained. The drop in CE revenue had also been more than compensated for by the rise in ICE revenue. And the ICE revenue had been growing at a very healthy clip – 24 percent in FY14, and 36.4 percent in 1Q15. To value the ICE segment at 4.4 times earnings, as the analyst did, was quite ridiculous.

Thus this was a crisis of confidence more than a crisis of business for Valuetronics – but a crisis nonetheless. And the sound investor would have seen this very pronounced loss of confidence in the company as unwarranted, and picked up some stock between 30 and 38 cents. As it turned out, not only did the Industrial and Commercial Electronics segment continue to boom, the company managed to turn around its Consumer Electronics segment as well, by adapting to change and moving on to higher-value products such as smart lighting systems. Something that both the market and analyst failed to take into account was the adaptability of the firm. It had been in business since 1992 in a fiercely competitive business (and listed since 2007). Change and adversity were nothing new to them.

As of 15 Feb 2018, Valuetronics was trading at 94 cents. If you had bought it at 38 cents, you would have made a total return of 202.7 percent[5] within slightly over three years. If you had been in the position to reinvest your dividends into Valuetronics stock to compound your returns, you would have done even better.

MY EXPERIENCE OF INVESTING IN CRISES

For me, crisis investing has been a key approach in stock investment. I buy promising growth stocks during crises, which could be particular to the stock or general. This approach has proven to be a winner over the decades. *I keep at least 20 per cent of my portfolio in cash, in preparation for an unforeseen crisis ahead.*

My current portfolio is made up entirely of profits gained from investing in mostly small and medium enterprises with promise. They were bought during downturns or crises and subsequently recovered to become multi-baggers, i.e. their value multiplied by three times or more. Their outperformance has enabled my portfolio to achieve a compounded annual return of around 15.5 per cent since 1990 when I set aside $200,000 of earlier gains as a base.

That base stood at $5 m at the end of 2010, twenty years later. I also received $1.4 m in dividends during the period. That is a total gain of $4.8 m + $1.4 m = $6.2 m[6], or a compound annual return of 18.9 percent, and implies a doubling of the portfolio value every four years. I've been myself surprised at those returns on my portfolio and perhaps for that reason, it has underperformed in the last seven years.

At the end of 2017, the portfolio, made up mainly of SGX-listed shares, had a value of $6.5 m and total dividends received had built up to $2.8 m. Original capital plus returns was $9.3 m. This represents a sharp deceleration in returns. Had I maintained the sizzling 18.9 percent compound returns, portfolio value plus dividends would have been $12.7 m in 2014 and a staggering $21.4 m in 2017.

My compounded returns since 1990 on the $200,000 base have thus been considerably muted. The lower returns in the last seven years (from 2011 to 2017) have been partly due to losses on S-chips or China-based companies listed in Singapore, which have had very poor corporate governance and let down many investors badly. Since 2005, I have lost close to a quarter million dollars on stocks such as China Sun Biotech, Fibre Chem, China Hongxing, China Milk, China Paper and China Sky. They are all worthless now. Recently, in 2015 and 2016, there have been problems with Pacific Andes, China Fishery, Noble and Rickmers Maritime, putting another $250,000 in deficit category.

But we have to move on as investors. Successful individuals are those who work at healing the scars of past mistakes and learn from them; they are not afraid to try again. Some of these stocks mentioned were promising but high-risk ventures. Investors were done in by fraud or by poor business and debt management, or by a sharp downturn in the industry concerned. This takes us back to the point in Chapter 5 about ascertaining whether we can trust the people who run a firm. We have to be particularly careful when the company is from another country with very different ways of doing business. The company directors may be unfamiliar to local investors, and it may also be difficult to independently assess their integrity and track record. In such cases, it is probably better to stay away.

Among the good performers in my portfolio is Golden Agri, which I accumulated during the Asian Financial Crisis in 1997. The portfolio also did well with Malaysian shares like RHB

Bank and Kulim Plantations, and Straits Trading, also bought during the Asian Financial Crisis and the Clob saga, and sold in 2007, multiplying values between 4 times and 7.5 times. More recently, AEM Holdings and Best World have been star performers, with multi-bagger returns. The portfolio is also sitting on good returns with technology stocks like Sunningdale, Valuetronics, Sunright, UMS and Hi-P. In medical care, HMI has been outstanding in recent years while Kingsmen Creatives and Boustead Singapore have been good investments too.

I am confident that my approach of buying growth stocks in crises, or the GSIC strategy, works well in the long term. It is superior to other investment methods like pure value investing, or buying blue chips and averaging down. I go for companies that have good business models and management, whose debt is manageable and cashflow is positive. There must be sizeable 'moats' around the businesses so they cannot be run over or duplicated that easily.

When do I sell my stocks? This seems to be one of the great conundrums of investing, but I proffer a fairly simple answer: when they are overvalued. It is simply the opposite of the reason why one would *buy* a stock, a car, an electric cooker. Of course establishing whether a stock is overvalued is less simple.

Sometimes only a handful of stocks in the market are overvalued; at other times, the majority of stocks are trading significantly above their intrinsic worth.

I usually sell during euphoric times like the 2007 run-up in equities which brought the Straits Times index to almost 4000 points, a historic high. Many stocks were overvalued.

Some of these stocks were gradually repurchased during the massive global stock market/economic rout in 2008/9. This was one of the opportunities of a lifetime to buy more growth stocks than ever at low, low prices. Some of those stocks were gradually sold in 2017, during the Trump rally with spillover effects in our market.

Other stocks were sold when their fair values had been reached or were exceeded. The key here is fair value. One has to decide what is the fair value of a stock, based on its fundamentals and growth prospects. Fair values can be adjusted over time, as the company exceeds or underperforms your expectations. But the discipline has to be there to sell a stock when it has outrun its fundamentals and has become overvalued.

Another important time to sell is when one no longer has a positive view on a company's quality or prospects. Despite our best efforts, there will surely be times when we misjudge a company – perhaps the Board is not as honest or competent as we thought, or the long-term prospects for the business have dimmed. If our investment thesis (grounds for investing) no longer exists, then it is only logical to sell. This might mean taking a loss, which is no doubt painful. But in investing as in life, we cannot succeed if we do not face up to our mistakes, bite the bullet and cut our losses.

For a more detailed discussion on how to value a stock, please see Chapter 8.

---

1 Raffles Medical underwent a 3-for-1 stock split on 11 May 2016, meaning each share was split into three and the number of shares you held would have tripled. Share prices have been adjusted for meaningful comparison.

2 Assuming the investor subscribed to his full entitlement (without receiving any excess rights) in the 20-for-100 rights issue at $1.28 which went ex on 3 Jul 2017.

3 Raffles Medical, op. cit.

4 VALUETRONICS: "Losing the light; Initiate with SELL," says Maybank. Nextinsight.net, 14 Oct 2014, https://www.nextinsight.net/index.php/story-archive-mainmenu-60/924-2014/9136-valuetronics-losing-the-light-initiate-with-sell-says-maybank

5 After factoring in 67 HK cents of total dividends (converted into SGD at an exchange rate of 1 HKD=0.174 SGD, which was roughly the mid-point of the exchange rate range during the years when those dividends were paid), as well as a 1-for-10 bonus share issue in May 2017. Capital gain was 172 percent, and dividend yield 30.7 percent.

6 I treat all dividends received from 1990 onwards as additional return (separate from the value of the portfolio) as I did not reinvest my dividends from that point on. This is because I had other commitments such as raising three children, supporting other family members, insurance policies, building up the family cash reserves and paying off mortgages.

   I also did not, in effect, inject any significant fresh capital during the period as my salary went towards these other commitments as well. Thus my current portfolio is by and large built up from that $200,000 base in 1990. At times, the portfolio did borrow from family cash reserves, but these 'loans' were repaid as soon as possible. Such 'loans' were mostly during crises and used to buy stocks at cheap valuations, or to average down.

CHAPTER 8

COMMON SENSE STOCK VALUATION

The crux of value investing is to identify companies or businesses that are undervalued by the market. The market is supposed to be efficient but at times, it misses the woods for the trees. Stocks go out of favour and into long periods of neglect and decline. That's bad news for those who bought the stocks at higher levels, but it is also an opportunity for value investors looking for bargains.

There is a lot of literature out there on value investing principles. The doyen of all investors, Warren Buffett, says one should be greedy when others are fearful. Conversely, one should be fearful when others are throwing caution to the wind. I buy stocks with good business models and governance during periods of crisis or neglect; the time to sell is when euphoria in the market has driven a stock price far above what its earnings prospects and balance sheet would justify.

However, this is easier said than done. A good investor has to do a lot of homework. Before you put any money in a company, you have to read as much as possible about its business model, competitive advantages, management and corporate governance.

Most of us are small investors, so we don't want a management that has no consideration for minority shareholders.

If you are satisfied with the basics of the business and its drivers, you can start looking at other fundamentals like the balance sheet and the profit or loss track record. Then you compare the profitability to the price through ratios such as price-earnings or PE ratio, and balance sheet to price through ratios such as price to book or P/B ratio – all these to establish if the price is lower, greater or equal to intrinsic value (the true or fair value of the stock based on the fundamentals). There is a whole morass of financial metrics and jargon that makes a beginner feel like tearing his hair out. *"Can you put in simple layman terms how to value a company?", you might ask. That is exactly what I seek to do in this chapter.*

For avoidance of doubt, when I say a stock is 'cheap' or 'expensive', what I mean is that it is undervalued or overvalued vis-a-vis its fundamentals – and *not* that its sticker price is low or high. As investors, it would be foolhardy for us to call one stock 'cheap' just because it is trading at a low sticker price, say 20 cents a share, and another 'expensive' just because its sticker price is $20. The former may be a shabby business run by mediocre management and heavily in debt, a business that has little competitive advantage and can be muscled out by its competitors at any time. Its intrinsic value may actually be less than 3 cents a share. The latter may be a world-class enterprise with a superb management team, cutting-edge intellectual property and a rock-solid balance sheet. Its intrinsic value may be $30 or $40 a share.

THE CHICKEN RICE RESTAURANT MODEL (CRRM)
Cut Through The Numbers With Your Common Sense

Many people, in their efforts to learn about stock investing, get turned off or intimidated by the sheer array of financial terms, elements and ratios involved. Sometimes they drown in the numbers, which seem to bring more confusion than clarity to the investor's mind.

Fret not – you do not need to understand the financial statements like an accountant to be a good investor. What you need is a strong understanding of the fundamentals and then exercise your Common Sense (keep it strong and fit!) to strongly grasp *what these numbers actually mean in reality*. To comprehend an investment in straightforward terms, I always fit it into the analogy of buying a chicken rice restaurant. Thus this part of my methodology is called the Chicken Rice Restaurant Model (CRRM).

It is grounded in the simple fact that buying a stock as an investor (rather than as a trader or speculator) means purchasing a stake in a business. A chicken rice restaurant is one of the simplest examples of a business, and will clarify in our minds exactly what we are looking for in the course of the investing endeavour.

Let's say you have a favourite Hainanese chicken rice restaurant called Wong's. Old Mr Wong is already in his 70s, and would like to retire. But his children are not keen to take over. Thus he is looking for a buyer to take over his enterprise. It is one of your favourite restaurants – you have enjoyed his chicken rice since you were a child, and you know it has a strong and loyal clientele.

For simplicity of understanding, we will simulate very low numbers in the restaurant's finances (yes, we will sacrifice a bit of realism for simplicity – with due apologies to Mr Wong). Let's say the restaurant's annual net profit is, on average, $1,000 a year. It has no cash in the bank and also no debt.

You know that it is a very stable business (but with little growth). Does it have an investment 'moat' and can it hold its own against the competition? Clearly it does and it can – there are numerous other eateries around it, but it has done brisk business all these years. There is just something about their chicken and their sauce that others can't replicate.

How much would you be willing to pay for the restaurant? (a) $1,000, (b) $5,000, (c) $10,000, (d) $15,000, (e) $20,000?

Here's a Common Sense take on the issue. There is good reason why the average valuation for stocks is usually 10-15 times net earnings (popularly known as *price-earnings or PE ratio*). It would not make sense for an owner to sell his stable business to you for less than 10-15 years of earnings. If all that you were willing to offer him was five years of earnings, he might as well keep the cash cow for himself and his children. A business owner would rarely accept less than 10-15 years of earnings unless he was desperate, or his business was in decline.

Thus it would be sensible to pay $10,000 for the chicken rice restaurant. Of course if the owner is prepared to let it go for less, all the better for you.

Now what if the restaurant held $5,000 in its corporate bank account and had no debt? Provided the owner agrees not to withdraw the cash, that $5,000 of net cash (cash minus debt) will be yours once you buy the eatery. Thus you can treat the net cash as a *discount* on your purchase price. It would be reasonable for you to pay $10,000 + $5,000 = $15,000 for the restaurant now. In effect, the cost to you would be only $10,000, as there is a $5,000 discount (the net cash held by the business which would become yours after the takeover). In stock market parlance, you would be paying a *PE ratio ex cash*[1] of 10 (10 times annual earnings after treating net cash on balance sheet as discount).

If the owner was only asking for $10,000 for the restaurant, then it would be a steal. As there is a $5,000 discount in the form of net cash, you would effectively be paying only $5,000 for the business, or five years of earnings for a stable business (5 times PE ex cash).

Now what if the restaurant, on top of the $5,000 net cash, also owned the real estate that it occupies? And this real estate was worth $10,000? Again if the owner agrees not to sell the property, it would become another discount on your purchase because the property would become yours after you buy the restaurant. In that case it would be reasonable to pay $10,000 + $5,000 + $10,000 = $25,000 for the restaurant.

Suppose the owner was in desperate need of cash, and agreed to sell it to you for only $15,000 – merely the value of the net cash and physical property. In that case, the *operating business* of the restaurant, i.e. selling chicken rice, and its intangible assets – its brand and recipes – would be yours for free. Believe it or not, there are actually listed companies selling for such valuations. Sometimes they are great buys, perhaps because the market has totally neglected them and underpriced them. But at other times they are *not* good buys as the company's integrity may be in doubt, or there may be some other major negative such as a massive lawsuit against them.

Now let's imagine a quite different situation. Suppose that instead of having $5,000 in net cash, the restaurant had $5,000 in net *debt*, meaning that it had $5,000 more debt than cash. In that case, the debt would become a *liability* to you[2] after you take over the establishment. Thus Common Sense would dictate that you treat it as a *premium* on your purchase. Imagine also that the restaurant did not own any physical property or any other durable asset of significant value. In that case you would be wise not to pay more than $10,000 (10 years' earnings) - $5,000 (net debt) = $5,000. The effective cost to you would still be $10,000 as the net debt is as good as a premium you are paying on your purchase price.

One final scenario. Imagine that Wong's business is booming. It is becoming tough to get a table, and he has opened two new outlets that have made a promising start and could increase the company's rate of earnings growth to 50 percent annually for the next five years. Even if you are conservative in your estimates, you are confident that the business can grow at a compounded annual growth rate of at least 30 percent a year for the next five years. In that case net profit will be 271 percent higher after five years. Another popular metric used by stock investors is *price-earnings to growth* or *PEG ratio*. It is the stock's price-earnings or PE ratio divided by its projected growth over a specified period of time. It makes sense to compare PE ratio to projected growth rate as a company's growth prospects obviously affect its intrinsic, objective value.

In stock markets, a PEG ratio of less than 1 is typically considered cheap.

Thus if Wong's chicken rice business is most likely to grow 30 percent compounded every year for the next five years (for simplicity, we shall assume zero cash, debt and physical property on the balance sheet), it would be attractive to pay anything less than 30 times earnings (30 years of net profit). This suggests that anything less than $30,000 would be a nice price. At $29,000, you might be paying 29 times earnings based on the previous financial year's (FY) profit, but if the net profit does grow 271 percent in total after five years, your purchase price will be only 7.8 times the annual earnings five years from now (it could be even lower as you have based this computation on a conservative estimate of future earnings). With that in mind, a price of $29,000 (29 times last FY's earnings) is clearly attractive.

Applying The CRRM To Actual Stocks

The time was early June, 2016. Avi-Tech Electronics, an electronics manufacturer and service provider, had just achieved a seventh consecutive quarter of profitability. It was yet another firm step in its path to recovery after several years of losses caused by an overseas venture that had not worked out. The company had recorded net profit for the third quarter of the FY ending June 2016 (3Q16) of $1.4 m. For the first nine months of FY16, it had raked in $4.9 m of earnings and paid $1.4 m of that to shareholders as a dividend. In FY15, the previous financial year, it had earned $6.6 m and paid out $4.5 m of that to shareholders.

Not only was the profitability showing solid signs of improvement, the company also had a rock-solid balance sheet. As of 3Q16, it had total assets of $52.0 m, which included cash and bank balances of $4.9 m, fixed and call deposits of $22.8 m and held-to-maturity financial assets of $1.2 million. Group's total liabilities, meanwhile, stood at $7.9 m, which included debt of only $1.2 m.

Very firm and encouraging numbers with tremendous improvement in profitability for the last seven quarters as a whole, and yet the share price still lagged far behind the fundamentals. This was likely due in no small part to the fear of investors because the company was on the Singapore Exchange watch-list – a list of companies that would face delisting if their performance did not improve. However, in its irrational fear, the market failed to realise that with *one* more quarter of profitability, the company would have largely met the requirements for removal from the watch-list.

So let us apply the CRRM to see how cheap or expensive Avi-Tech's stock was as of 8 June, 2016. We will be working the numbers in a very similar way to how we did for Wong's Chicken Rice Restaurant, but now we will be working on a *per share* basis as it makes the numbers easy to compare with the share price (price per share).

Avi-Tech's numbers
Price per share = 23.5 cents

Net cash per share = 16.2 cents[3]

If you treat net cash per share as a discount on your purchase,
Effective amount you are paying per share
= 23.5 cents – 16.2 cents = 7.3 cents.

Earnings per share (based on first nine months of FY16 alone, without even counting earnings for the upcoming fourth quarter) = 2.83 cents.

Thus if you bought it at the market price of 23.5 cents, you would have been paying only 7.3 cents/2.83 cents = 2.6 times earnings.

Bear in mind, we are talking about 2.6 times of only *nine months' earnings* and not even a full year!

If this were the chicken rice restaurant we were talking about earlier, it would have been the rough equivalent of Mr Wong selling you the restaurant for $7,600 when it had $5,000 in the bank, no debt and $1,000 in annual earnings[4] with good growth prospects. 2.6 times earnings ex cash for a stable business with bright prospects[5]! For that to happen, Mr Wong would have had to be (a) out of his mind, (b) desperate or (c) your best friend on the Earth.

Such an absurdly cheap valuation! Yet the stock market sometimes actually gives us such offers. It is obvious that the market's efficiency (in pricing stocks accurately) is far from perfect, contrary to what the extreme advocates of the Efficient Market Hypothesis tell us.

Thus, the CRRM tells us that on 8 June 2016, Avi-Tech Electronics was a 'Buy' at the market price of 23.5 cents.

What happened after that?

The stock climbed steadily to double at 47 cents in less than a year (April 2017), and stood at 52.5 cents as of 16 March 2018 – a 123 percent capital gain if you had bought it. On top of that, the company would have paid you 3.8 cents a share in dividends – a further 16.2 percent return. A total return of 139.2 percent in less than two years. You would be a pretty prosperous restaurant owner.

Chart 8.1: Avi-Tech Electronics: Five-year chart as of 14 June, 2018

DIVIDEND YIELD

Another important metric to look at is *dividend yield*, which is the annual percentage return (on your cost) that an investor gets from dividends alone. There is the historical or trailing yield (based on what was paid in the previous financial year), and the forward yield (based on what is likely to be paid going forward).

The formula for dividend yield is: *Total dividends per share in a financial year/Share Price*

As of June 2016, Avi-Tech had declared and paid out 2.2 cents per share (out of a total of 2.83 cents in net profit) in that financial year. With the final quarterly result to come and business going well hitherto, it was likely that they would declare one more dividend for the FY. If they were to earn 0.8 cents per share for the final quarter (as they did in the third quarter) and pay out a similar proportion, the final quarter would see an approximate 0.6 cent dividend. Thus one could expect a total dividend of 2.2 cents + 0.6 cents = 2.8 cents per share for the year.

Thus estimated dividend yield (a combination of trailing and forward yield) would be = Total dividends per share/Share price
= 2.8 cents/ 23.5 cents
= 11.9 percent

That would have been a superb dividend yield. Based on the strong business momentum and positive industry conditions, it was also likely that an investor would be able to receive at least this level of yield for the next couple of financial years. As it turned out, Avi-Tech declared a 1 cent per share final dividend for FY2016 ending June 2016, making their dividend yield even higher at 13.6 percent. Of course one had to ask whether the company would continue to pay investors their fair share in the future. The solid track record of Avi-Tech in this respect gave reason for assurance to investors.

Of course, dividends are not everything. Sometimes it may be worthwhile to invest in a firm whose stock pays a very modest dividend yield, e.g. 1 or 2 percent. This may be because the company is retaining most of its earnings for expansion, or because the stock price has risen so much that the dividend yield has naturally diminished. However, if you are convinced that the company's earnings will rise very strongly in future – making current valuations still attractive – it may be a good buy.

Dividends are important for providing passive income to investors, especially full-time investors or retirees. Thus it makes good sense to balance high-growth, low-dividend yield stocks with low-growth, high-dividend yield counters.

If one can get a high-growth stock with a high forward dividend yield, all the better! AEM Holdings is a good example. On 27 June 2017, the semiconductor equipment solutions outfit was trading at $2.34 a share. It had already announced $4.1 m in net profit (9.47 cents a share after accounting for potential dilution from stock options) for 1Q17, an explosive growth of 1,616 percent year on year. Furthermore, the company provided guidance of $17.5 m profit before tax for the first nine months of FY17, which would roughly translate to $14.5 m after tax or 33.5 cents per share. As the firm had a dividend policy of paying not less than 25 percent of net profit to shareholders, an investor in AEM could expect at least 8.4 cents per share in dividend or a 3.6 percent dividend yield based on the first nine months of the FY alone. That would be a very handsome yield for a growth stock. With its superb growth, there was the potential for even better payouts down the line – and so it proved. The company achieved splendid results in its fourth quarter as well, and paid out a final dividend of 6.5 cents, taking the full-year dividend to 12 cents a share. If you had bought it at $2.34 in June 2017[6,] you would be looking at a yield of 5.1 percent – similar to what some real estate investment trusts were paying out, but with the promise of exciting growth still to come.

A word to the wise, though: be careful not to take dividend yield at face value. You must ask yourself where that yield is coming from, and whether it can be sustained. For instance, is the succulent yield of 12 percent in a given year boosted by exceptional, one-off earnings like the sale of a building? Is the dividend paid out from profits, or merely cashflow? The latter is an important point because some entities such as Singapore-listed business trusts are allowed to pay dividends based on cashflow, which may be higher than profit. Cashflow does not take into account depreciation charges[7], which reflect past capital expenditure (capex) and are an indication of likely future capex needs as well. For instance, a business trust that owns a port may be able to pay 5 cents a share in dividend for the next five years based on cashflow even though it is earning only 3 cents a share in net profit. Five years later, it may need to undertake massive capex (for instance, replacing old port equipment) and will need to slash dividends as cash is drained and it has not been setting aside cash for these heavy expenditures. In such cases, dividend yield for the last few years can be a very cosmetic reflection of value.

PRICE/FREE CASHFLOW (P/FCF)

Price over Free Cashflow is another fairly basic and very useful valuation metric. Instead of focusing on earnings like the PE ratio (or PE ex cash) does, P/FCF zeroes in on *free cashflow (FCF)* – the cash generated by the company's operations minus capital expenditures (capex). FCF represents the cash that a company is able to generate after spending the money required to maintain or expand its asset base.

FCF is arguably more important than earnings because the cash generated by a company's earnings can be chewed up by heavy capex, leaving little or even no cash to put in the bank, pursue growth opportunities or pay to shareholders. For instance, a semiconductor firm may need to spend more and more on each new generation of fabrication plants. An egg farming company may have its land reacquired by the government and need to buy new land and construct new facilities in a new location.

Price over Free Cashflow can be calculated as follows: Market capitalisation[8]/Free cashflow

Thus a company that produces operating cashflow of $50 m and incurs capex of $25 m generates FCF of $25 m. If its market capitalisation is $250 m, then its P/FCF is $250 m/$25 m = 10 times. The lower the P/FCF, the lower the company's valuation and the cheaper the stock seems. Of course, that does not necessarily signal a good buy. One needs to consider other factors and danger signs – see "Caveats to the Chicken Rice Restaurant Model" below.

An investor should also be mindful that free cashflow can be manipulated by companies, for example by delaying payments to suppliers or holding off purchases of inventory.

CAVEATS TO THE CHICKEN RICE RESTAURANT MODEL

While it is good to have the financial metrics explained in a simple manner, we must be cautious not to take a simplistic view. Thus it's important to apply a bit of critical thinking to our Common Sense and be clear about the difference between buying the hypothetical chicken rice restaurant and investing in a listed company.

1. In the Chicken Rice Restaurant Model, we buy the entire restaurant and control it. But when we buy a stock, it usually will be a non-controlling stake.

We cannot, for instance, just withdraw the company's net cash and put it into our personal bank account. Neither can we dictate the amount of dividends that is paid out to stockholders, or the salary and bonuses of the CEO.

We must study the track record of the firm as a *listed* company, not just as an operating business. As a listed company, does it have a long and solid track record of distributing a fair share of earnings and returning excess cash to shareholders? Does it overpay the directors and top executives in fees, salaries, bonuses and stock options? A desired state of affairs would be if the directors and executives are paid reasonable fees, salaries and bonuses and they also hold significant amounts of stock. That way, their interests are more aligned with minority shareholders. If healthy dividends are paid out or the stock price rises, both you and they will benefit.

There is also the paramount issue of trust. When you do not control how the company is run and the accounts kept, you must have a high degree of confidence that the head honchos are trustworthy. To learn how to make this assessment, please see Chapters 5 and 9.

If a listed company lacks integrity, then it doesn't matter how 'cheap' or 'undervalued' the stock seems. The value could be imaginary.

2. Beware the value trap – look for imminent catalysts

Sometimes there really is tremendous value in a company, like a well-located building or a large pile of cash on its balance sheet that does not seem to be captured in the stock price. In extreme cases, some companies even trade below their net cash or net current asset value. In the latter case, it means that the stock price is less than the current assets (such as receivables and cash) minus all liabilities (such as payables and all debt), divided by total number of shares. In theory you would be getting all the real estate and equipment (non-current assets) plus the operating business for free.

Then there are times when a company makes quite consistent profits but trades at a ridiculously low PE ratio, like 2-3 years' earnings.

Not all of the above scenarios equate to a good buy. Why? Because very often the latent value is very unlikely to be unlocked – they are often value traps.

One possible reason for the value being immobilised is that the bosses (who may also be controlling shareholders) are selfish characters who refuse to pay a reasonable dividend (while receiving huge salaries and directors' fees). Sometimes they have a mountain of cash on their books, but they refuse to return a good chunk of it to shareholders even though they have no expansion plans or other good reasons to hold on to it. Then there are companies which have rather hare-brained ideas for business expansion or acquisitions, and end up squandering the cash.

Having said all that, you can try to unlock a value trap if you are brave. There are activist investment funds that write open letters to pressure companies to unlock value for shareholders. One such activist fund, Quarz Capital Management, wrote to retailer and real estate developer Metro Holdings to return excess cash to shareholders in 2016. It is more difficult to act on your own as a retail investor but you can speak up at AGMs persistently or band together with other minority shareholders to pressure a company online or offline.

Be prepared for a hostile reception from the Board and a hard slog with no assurance of results. But sometimes if you are persistent enough, the value trap can be unfastened. Once when

I asked at an AGM why the company paid zero dividends despite having steady earnings, I was told, "If you want dividends, why don't you invest in a REIT (Real Estate Investment Trust)?" But after a few years of pressure from shareholders, the company finally started paying dividends.

If you would rather save yourself the trouble – avoid such companies!

Sometimes, even when a listed company has a healthy business and honest, fair directors, the stock may remain sluggish for years due to its very low profile in the market or a lack of excitement. If you don't want to wait forever for a stock to perform, then look for those with *imminent and probable catalysts*. It could come in the form of probable improved earnings and higher dividends for the coming quarters, which the market has not priced in yet. We can anticipate this by studying the company and industry closely, or meeting with management at an AGM or results briefing. For instance, we might hear from a friend in the industry that the demand for a food manufacturer's product is likely to boom due to industry trends. We might visit the construction site of a real estate developer and find that their new office building is almost complete and we anticipate a substantial boost to earnings that the market has not woken up to. Or in our meeting with the directors of an electronics firm, we might get a sense of an excellent synergy between the company and its latest acquisition, which the market has yet to appreciate.

Of course we have to be careful to differentiate between objective evaluations of probable outcomes and wild, fanciful speculation. Invest based on what you *logically believe* is likely to happen grounded on *facts*, rather than what you dream or hope will happen.

Certain catalysts are probable but may be very far from imminent. For instance, a general offer by a major shareholder to buy all the shares that she does not own. In your own mind, this may be a probable scenario due to the inclinations and past behaviour of this major shareholder – but that does not mean it will happen anytime soon. There are times when minority shareholders have to wait a decade or more! If the stock provides a good dividend yield (dividend per share divided by share price) of 5 percent or more, then it makes it easier and more worthwhile to wait. But do take into account the opportunity cost – the potential profit that you forgo from alternative investments that you could be making.

3. The listed company probably experiences different industry dynamics from the Chicken Rice Restaurant

Not every listed company is in an industry as stable as staple food. A listed firm may be in a highly cyclical business, such as real estate or shipping. In such a case, looking at the last three or even five years of earnings may not give a good reflection of what the earnings capacity of the company will be for the next few years.

Many companies are also more prone to disruption than a chicken rice eatery. It is difficult for technology to make a much loved local food redundant. But we cannot say the same for a company that makes film for cameras (disrupted by digital cameras), a newspaper business (troubled by new media and the Internet), a hotel business (affected by Airbnb) or even a dominant taxi business (hammered by Uber). When we invest in any business, we need to stay alert for trends and developments that could make our company's product or service less relevant, or even totally obsolete.

Every business experiences different risk factors. Sometimes it could be the same risk factors but to different degrees. A bank, for example, is subjected to the risk of interest rates falling, which pull down its net interest margins[9]. A REIT which owns properties outside the country where it is listed is vulnerable to currency fluctuations. And enterprises that operate in politically volatile regions can see severe disruptions due to revolutions and civil war. We can get a sense of the risk factors inherent in each business by reading the IPO prospectus (section on risk factors disclosure) and the annual report, in particular the Chairman/ CEO's statements. Reading about the relevant countries of operation and the industry as a whole is equally helpful.

4. The value of some companies' assets can be very subjective

Net cash and physical property, which were assets mentioned in the restaurant scenarios above, are very easy to value on an objective basis (unless there is fraud – please see the relevant sections in Chapters 5 and 9 on how to identify a less-than-honest company).

You can't get an asset more straightforward than cash. In the case of real estate, as it is an asset that is widely traded, it is not difficult for an established valuer to provide a credible assessment of what it is worth. If the company were to be liquidated, it would also be relatively easy to realise the value by selling the real estate.

This is not quite so with, say, industrial machinery. An electronics manufacturing company may record their esoteric machinery on the balance sheet as being worth $10 m. But it is hard to objectively value this asset, as this kind of machinery may not be as actively traded. Worse, it might even become obsolete due to technological advancement.

Another instance of an asset with subjective value is goodwill. Goodwill value typically arises during a business acquisition. When one company buys another company, it may pay more money than the target company's book value for certain intangible assets such as brand name, customer base, and patents. These assets are known as goodwill[10] and their value is certainly not easy to assess unless you are an expert.

If you do not have the expertise to assess these assets, then it would be wise to regard their book value (official value on the balance sheet) with a pinch of salt. If you would like to focus mainly on the cash on balance sheet (the easiest asset to value), then you can place greater weight on metrics such as PE ex cash.

This would be an opportune time to discuss another popular valuation metric – price to book ratio, or P/B ratio. This is the ratio of the stock price (price per share) to the book value (official accounting value of all the assets of the company minus all the liabilities) per share.

Many investors place as much or even more importance on this metric as they do the PE or price-earnings ratio. It is often said that one should buy a stock that is trading below book value. In the minds of many investors, this provides a margin of safety because theoretically, the book value or net asset value per share is what they could get back on a per-share basis if the whole company were to be liquidated. In theory, the bigger the discount to book value, the better the investment.

Unfortunately in real life, it does not always work like that. As discussed, some companies are frauds, others are value traps, and in some other cases, the value of the assets is highly subjective. Thus even a massive discount to book value, like 60 or 70 percent, does not automatically mean a stock is a good buy.

The reverse is also true. Trading *above* book value does not necessarily mean that a stock is *not* a good buy. I don't think it is a good idea to be too much of a Scrooge or extreme value investor in the sense that one will only invest in a company when it is trading below book value. We should not only think like scavengers out to strip off a company's assets at an auction; we should also look to buy a great *business* with its fabulous expertise, processes, brand, culture, customer relationships and earnings potential. A good company is so much more than just its cash balances, receivables, building and so on.

In my mind, a true value investor looks for value not only on the balance sheet. Many of the above attributes of the company such as customer relationships are often not even on the balance sheet. While I have said that the value of such intangible assets is subjective, it doesn't mean that there is no value. For instance, I trust you would agree that if an electronics manufacturer has strong, decades-long relationships with Samsung, Intel and Bose, those relationships are substantial assets. We should take it into consideration and ascribe our own value to it, cautiously and in conjunction with our evaluation of the firm's hard assets.

Put another way, the value of a company is not only its liquidation value, it is also its ability to generate earnings in the next five, ten, twenty years. Yes, we can sometimes make money by buying into so-so companies that are trading at deep discounts to book value or pitiful PE ratios. But we experience the magic of business when we buy into a *superb* business at *reasonable valuations*, for instance 10-15 times PE ex cash and 2 times book value.

It is also worth noting that for companies in different industries, the most salient measures of assets would also be different. For instance, for a property firm, net tangible assets (NTA) per share is usually the most salient as its most important assets are usually its real estate. For an insurance company though, embedded value is very high up on the priority list. This is because one of an insurer's most valuable assets is typically the insurance policies, effectively contracts which it has signed with its customers. Future income for the insurer comprises premiums paid by policyholders whilst future costs include claims paid to policyholders and various other expenses. The difference, combined with income on and release of statutory reserves, represents future profit. Embedded value measures the value of the insurer by adding today's value of the existing business (future earnings discounted for time, on the basis that a dollar in the future is worth less than a dollar today) to the market value of net assets[11].

5. Be flexible

Some investors have hard and fast rules that they stick to in deciding on their investments. But I think it is best to be flexible. For example, what level of debt is acceptable? Some companies have businesses which are more capital-intensive, so they need to borrow to augment their own equity base. But the returns going forward could be handsome, which makes the risk of a leveraged balance sheet worthwhile.

Should you invest only in blue chips? People tell you that only blue chips are "safe" and every other company is "risky". Is that really true? Why can't a small- or medium-sized business be solidly run and steadily profitable? Have you not seen a little coffee shop or medium-sized hospital like that?

6. Beware the Pie in the Sky; don't overpay for potential growth

Estimating a company's growth potential in the years ahead is a tricky affair. This is what analysts do; they estimate the revenues in the quarters and years ahead and then work down to the net profit level. If there is good growth ahead, then the stock is likely to do well and outperform the general market.

But sometimes forecasts go very wrong. The huge profits that are anticipated turn out to be just a Pie in the Sky. It is important to not get carried away with exciting growth stories and overpay for them. This is why I stress paying reasonable valuations for a superb business. Frequently the market demands 30, 50 or even over 100 times historical earnings for an exciting growth company. Great expectations are built into such price levels, especially those higher than 40. If the company fails to deliver on those expectations, the stock will come crashing down to earth.

But again, even if a company has good growth prospects, one has to estimate what its fair value should be. Look at ratios like price-to-earnings, PE versus growth, net asset value or net tangible assets, dividend yield and the potential to increase dividend in future. But how do you find stocks that are trading at attractive valuations? Checking on the ratios is not difficult. I use the ShareInvestor platform which offers good information on individual companies in the profile page and the fact sheet.

Most of the ratios are there and they are updated regularly, so that it is easy to form an accurate mental picture of a company's financial situation and track record on earnings and dividends, and valuations. There are also stock screeners on ShareInvestor, the SGX website (StockFacts tool), Finviz (for US stocks) and many other websites that enable you to search for stocks based on various parameters such as low PE ratios and high dividend yields. The difficulty is knowing when to buy and sell.

I am at heart a value investor, but I do glance at the historical pattern of the stock's price movement, especially over the last ten to twenty years. I think this is useful in giving you an idea of what the company and its shares have been through and the likely investor sentiment towards a particular stock. After all, the investing game is also a psychological one. How a stock does is what the crowds think it should do or want it to do. Looking at the charts sometimes allows you to make better decisions on the entry and exit points for your investment.

Once you have identified a stock with growth potential, it is a question of when to take a position. The valuation ratios have to be right for you and the margin of safety must be significant. For example, you would normally want a relatively low PE ratio, discount to NAV and attractive dividend yield. Such values can sometimes be found in normal markets but they are generally more available during major crises. These are black swan events that come once every five years or so.

MORE ESOTERIC/COMPLEX MEASURES OF VALUE

When we read analyst reports, we might encounter other, more complex valuation metrics. It is easy to get intimidated or confused by them, but my advice is – don't be. An investor can make good decisions with the simpler measures such as the price-earnings and price-to-book ratios.

But if you have the aptitude and inclination to learn the more esoteric metrics such as EV/EBITDA (Enterprise Value over Earnings before Interest, Taxes, Depreciation and Amortisation) and Discounted Cashflow (DCF), go right ahead. This book shall deal only briefly with these as I do not wish to overcomplicate the methodology and subject of investing. Also, there are plenty of good explanations on the Internet which you can easily access.

Enterprise Multiple (EV/EBITDA)

The Enterprise Multiple is calculated as follows.

First, we need to ascertain Enterprise Value, which is Market Capitalisation (current share price multiplied by total number of shares) + Value of Debt + Minority Interest + Preferred Shares – Cash and Cash Equivalents.

Then we divide this Enterprise Value by the Earnings before Interest, Taxes, Depreciation and Amortisation (EBITDA). This will give us the Enterprise Multiple or EV/EBITDA multiple.

The lower the Enterprise Multiple, the cheaper the stock can be said to be. Of course, we should take Enterprise Multiples based on historical earnings with a pinch of salt, as future earnings may not be as strong.

One strength of the EV/EBITDA metric over a plain PE ratio is that it takes into account a company's cash holdings and debt. But of course the PE *ex cash* ratio does this as well. Having said that, EV/EBITDA has the additional advantage of factoring in preferred shares. Preferred shares (also known as preferred stock) is more like debt than common stock (ordinary shares) as holders of preferred shares receive a fixed dividend and have a higher claim to a company's assets than ordinary shareholders do.

By excluding depreciation and amortisation, EV/EBITDA also eliminates the distorting effects of different depreciation policies by different companies. Some firms, for example, practise straight-line depreciation (depreciating the value of an asset over its useful life) while others practise accelerated depreciation (where they charge higher depreciation in early years and lower depreciation in later years). As depreciation is taken as a charge (deduction) in the profit and loss statement, companies that practise more conservative depreciation policies (such as accelerated depreciation) will report lower profits in the early years of the asset's life than those with more liberal depreciation policies. The Enterprise Multiple eliminates this effect.

However, a company's depreciation charges are not determined solely by depreciation policy. One firm might have a superior maintenance regime to another, allowing their machines to last longer and reducing capital expenditure. Some companies may be more frugal and use their machines for a longer time (for example an airline that uses its planes for fifteen years rather than ten), while there are firms that know how to build some of the equipment they use and therefore do not need to buy it.

For these reasons, EV/EBITDA does not provide a complete picture of a company and its stock valuation. It is best employed in conjunction with price-earnings ratio and other metrics.

Discounted Cashflow (DCF)

This book will not delve into the Discounted Cashflow methodology as I am of the opinion that it is an abstract valuation metric. For the lay investor, it is not necessary to use this metric to pick and choose the stocks that are good investments for the long term. When it comes to such highly mathematical methods of valuation, it would be worth considering the sagely words of Benjamin Graham from decades past, which will always remain relevant. Writing in *The Intelligent Investor in 1971-1972* (Fourth Edition), he observes that at the time that many growth stocks were trading at "such high prices in relation to past and current earnings, [analysts] recommending them have felt a special obligation to justify their purchase by fairly definite projections of expected earnings running far into the future. *Certain mathematical techniques of a rather sophisticated sort* have perforce been invoked to support the valuations arrived at... we must point out a troublesome paradox here, which is that *the mathematical valuations have become most prevalent precisely in those areas where one might consider them least reliable.* For the more dependent the valuation becomes on anticipations of the future – and the less it is tied to a figure demonstrated by past performance – the more vulnerable it becomes to possible miscalculation and serious error. A large part of the value found for a high-multiplier growth stock is derived from future projections which differ markedly from past performance – except perhaps in the growth rate itself. Thus it may be said that security analysts today find themselves compelled to become *most mathematical and 'scientific'* in the very situations which lend themselves *least auspiciously to exact treatment.*" [italics are mine]

I do not know which "mathematical techniques of a rather sophisticated sort" Graham was referring to, but DCF seems to fit such a description well. It involves highly complex calculations based on assumptions about a company's long-term free cashflow growth.

As Jason Zweig wrote in his commentary to Graham's *Intelligent Investor* (Fourth Edition), "Because advanced mathematics gives *the appearance of precision to the inherently iffy process of foreseeing the future*, investors must be *highly skeptical* of anyone who claims to hold any complex computational key to basic financial problems." Indeed Graham once said, "In 44 years of Wall Street experience and study, *I have never seen dependable calculations* made about common-stock values, or related investment policies, that *went beyond simple arithmetic or the most elementary algebra.* Whenever calculus is brought in, or higher algebra, you could take it as a *warning signal* that the operator was trying to *substitute theory for experience*, and usually also to *give to speculation the deceptive guise of investment.*"[12] (All italics in the paragraph are mine.)

---

1   Price earnings ratio excluding net cash, i.e. after you treat the company's net cash as a discount.

2   Most listed companies are limited companies, meaning that ordinary shareholders are not personally liable for the company's debt. The liability to shareholders is limited to what they have invested in or guaranteed to the company. Even if the firm becomes insolvent, its creditors cannot go after the ordinary shareholders for repayment. However, the company's debt can still be treated as a liability to you as an ordinary shareholder because it is a negative factor on the balance sheet which weighs down the value of your shares, and the interest payments are a drag on profit and dividends to you.

3   To calculate net cash per share, first I added up all the cash and cash-like assets (such as fixed and call deposits, and held-to-maturity financial assets) held by Avi-Tech. I then deducted all debt to obtain net cash. This number was divided by the total weighted number of shares in issue

(including all the stock options that had not yet been exercised, to be conservative) to obtain net cash per share.

4   Actually Avi-Tech was an even bigger bargain than that hypothetical chicken rice restaurant, as Avi-Tech was selling for 2.6 times of only *nine months'* earnings (not annual earnings) ex cash (after discounting net cash).

5   Avi-Tech was (and still is at the time of writing) well-positioned to ride economic megatrends such as the march towards autonomous cars, cloud computing, smart cities and the Internet of Things.

6   AEM Holdings awarded shareholders a 3-for-1 bonus issue in May 2018, meaning that you would receive three new shares for every one that you had. Thus if you wish to compare the share price before and after May 2018, you need to multiply the later share price by four as the total number of shares in issue had increased fourfold.

7   Depreciation is an accounting method of spreading out the cost of a capital expense (a productive asset, e.g. a factory or a vehicle) over a period of time on a company's books to better reflect the cost of that asset in each year. For instance, if you own a bakery and you buy a van for $30,000 to make deliveries, it would not be a good reflection of the van's cost to record it as a cost of $30,000 in that year. This is because that van can be used for at least ten years, so it effectively costs you $3,000 a year. Hence it would make sense to record its cost as $3,000 annually over ten years instead of $30,000 in one year. This is what we call depreciation. However, it does not reflect cashflow i.e. money flowing in and out of the business. The $30,000 might be paid in full upon purchase of the van; in subsequent years, $3,000 will be recorded as a cost in the accounts (deducted to calculate profit) but that $3,000 does not leave the company's cashflow as the van is already paid for.

8   Market capitalisation (or market cap) is the total value of all of a company's shares listed on the stock market. It is calculated by multiplying the market price per share by the total number of shares in issue.

9   Net interest margin (NIM) is a measure of the difference between the interest income generated by banks or other financial institutions and the amount of interest paid out to their lenders (for example, deposits), relative to the amount of their (interest-earning) assets. It is similar to the gross profit margin at non-financial companies.

10 Intuit Quickbooks website. https://quickbooks.intuit.com/ca/resources/finance-accounting/what-is-goodwill/

11 "Embedded value",Wikipedia https://en.wikipedia.org/wiki/Embedded_value

12 Benjamin Graham, *The Intelligent Investor* (Revised Edition), Harper Business Essentials, 1973. New material by Jason Zweig 2003.

CHAPTER 9

SCAMS, SHADY 'INVESTMENTS' AND YOUR RIGHTS

Around 2007, former Manchester United captain Bryan Robson appeared on TV with former Liverpool player Steve McMahon, exhorting all of us to "buy UK land". They were plugging a so-called investment company called Profitable Plots.

When faced with the global financial crisis of 2007 and 2008, Profitable Plots' land-based investment products suffered losses. To alleviate cashflow problems, their British directors John Nordmann and Timothy Goldring hatched a plan to get clients to pump money into the 'Boron scheme', which supposedly involved financing the sale of a fuel additive known as Boron CLS Bond to major corporations[1].

The company lured investors by promising 12.5 percent returns within six months, but ended up losing $3.1 million as a sizeable portion of the money ended up being used to pay the company's existing obligations instead. In 2010, as the promised dividend payments to investors were delayed again and again, twelve furious investors marched into the company's office to demand the repayment of $700,000 in total. An ugly confrontation ensued.[2]

Eventually Nordmann and Goldring were charged and convicted of cheating in Singapore's State Courts, and sentenced to eight years' and seven years' imprisonment respectively. But the victims did not get their money back.

It seems that virtually every month or even every week, a story like this emerges in most countries. People hear about these con jobs. Yet these devious tricks, repeated with often just cosmetic variations, manage to snare another few hundred or even thousands just a month later. It seems that greed, and the way it compromises our judgement, is an ingrained part of human nature. Beyond greed, there are other psychological tendencies such as our aspirations for success and social status; our love for family; insecurity; the fear of losing out; and crowd psychology. Scammers and unscrupulous business people are always looking to capitalise on these vulnerabilities.

For instance, the sales staff working for a Ponzi scheme[3] may wear Tom Ford suits and Lange and Sohn watches – exploiting our aspirations for the status that such possessions represent. They may parade their 'success stories' at their seminars, evoking our insecurities and fears of losing out. At some multi-level marketing (MLM) seminars, certain tactics are used to manipulate the crowd, such as the chanting of emotive slogans. I am not saying that every MLM scheme is fraudulent or manipulative – but some certainly are.

There is nothing wrong with aspiring to success and wealth. But we must be aware that at every turn, there is a ruthless opportunist out to exploit our aspirations to his own advantage. We need to strengthen our psychological defences, educate ourselves about their trickery, and always maintain a healthy level of scepticism and questioning.

We must not succumb to these deadly and devious entice-ments – or even our best-laid financial plans will lie in ruins.

This chapter will offer some guidelines to help protect you.

WHEN YOU SHOULD BE ESPECIALLY ON YOUR GUARD

Unregulated Investment Schemes And Organisations

As I already made clear in Chapter 2, even listed companies can effectively be scams or, more subtly, run in a way that will short-change small investors. But at least they are subject to regulations, which can be very stringent in a well-developed stock exchange. Such regulations, while imperfect, at least offer us a degree of protection.

But there is a host of purported 'investment' schemes and organisations that fall outside the ambit of regulators. These range from the above-mentioned land-banking firms to MLM schemes to 'gold buyback'; from cobalt mines to mushroom farms to the recent frenzy over cryptocurrencies like Bitcoin. Very often you get friends asking you to attend a seminar, or a salesman at a booth in a shopping mall approaching you to 'invest' in such schemes which are run by companies whose activities are not regulated by any government agency.

They might promise you rosy returns, but when things go wrong, you will often have no legal recourse or means to address your grievances. And even if you did – for instance if the fraudster was arrested and jailed – you would probably not get back a cent of your money. He would very likely have moved the assets offshore.

No shortage of crooks out there selling you paper empires

A special note on **Bitcoin (and other cryptocurrencies)** as interest in them has reached feverish levels from Manchester to Manila. There are very strong views in both the pro and anti camps. Certainly cryptocurrencies are part of a very promising technology known as blockchain, which holds immense potential to bring about exponential leaps in the efficiency of trade and business transactions.

But in my book, it would be very dangerous to regard such virtual, abstract assets as investments. You must always begin with the basics: what exactly are you buying? For me, investment is the reasoned, rational act of putting your capital in an asset that has clearly definable and measurable economic value. For instance, the value of a piece of land can be easily defined as its capacity to accommodate a shop and its tenants, and measured by the amount of monthly rent the tenants are likely to be willing to pay. If it is a painting by Monet, its economic value can be defined by its scarcity and the massive margin by which demand exceeds supply, which will underpin a hefty price that it can command at an auction. But how do you define and measure the value of a Bitcoin or other cryptocurrency? It exists only as a piece of data in a computer (and Bitcoin exchanges have been hacked and Bitcoins 'stolen'). How do we guarantee its scarcity? Yes, we are told that Bitcoins can only be produced by incredibly complex mathematical computations that require massive amounts of computer processing. But only a small handful of mathematical geniuses can understand this formula. If you don't, I would recommend that you don't get involved.

Buying into something that you are a thousand miles from understanding is not investment. It is speculation, and quite wild speculation at that. Also, there is no central authority to regulate Bitcoin. No one but a select few at most even know who created this mysterious 'asset'. If things go terribly wrong or cybercrime takes place to rob you of your virtual asset, you have no one to turn to for help.

Psychological Manipulation Is In Play

There are many tricks that con artists can play on you, some of which amount to virtual brainwashing. Crowd manipulation that whips up a large audience into something that resembles a religious fervour. The pulling of your emotional strings, like asking you if you wish to give your family a better life, using your friends to apply peer pressure on you, or flaunting wealth in front of you. Getting very charismatic individuals to speak.

When your emotional buttons are pressed heavily, your judgement will be severely compromised unless you have your defences up. Ask yourself some good, logical questions. For instance, if the product or asset the company is selling is so good, why is there a need to use so much psychological manipulation? Of course some sales tactics are normal and reasonable – but to go to such an extent to get 'investors' or 'members'?

The Returns Are Logically Unrealistic

Recall the 'Boron scheme' mentioned earlier in this chapter. It promised 12.5 percent returns in six months. That equates to 25 percent a year. This was in the 2007-2008 period when the ten-year US government bond yield, a well-known indicator of risk-free return, ranged between 3 and 5 percent a year. If the purveyors of Boron in the scheme could deliver a 25 percent annual return at a proportionately attractive level of risk (low risk-to-reward ratio), would they have taken the trouble to court an army of small-time investors? No – they would either have kept the investment opportunity for themselves or marketed it to savvy institutional and millionaire investors.

Sometimes the 'returns' are unrealistic in the sense of being impossibly stable. One recalls the greatest Ponzi scheme run by probably the biggest con artist of all time – Bernie Madoff. The once-respected American financier cheated some 24,000 clients out of US\$65 b in all. While his fund was in operation, it reported unusually consistent returns year after year, and even month after month. Harry Markopolos, a financial analyst and portfolio manager, told the Securities and Exchange Commission (SEC) in a submission that in an 87-month period (slightly over seven years), Madoff reported only three losing months while the broad-based S & P 500 index had twenty-eight. This produced a return stream that rose steadily upward at a nearly perfect 45-degree angle. The markets are far too volatile by nature for this to be possible. Later, he testified before Congress that this was like a baseball player batting .966 for the season and no one suspecting a cheat[4].

The truth is, one does not need an expert like Markopolos to tell us this. But most of Madoff's investors, so enamoured of the apparently glowing 'returns' and his stellar reputation, allowed their common logic to be shut down.

You should also be on your guard when a company's reported profit margins are much higher than their comparable competitors'. If there is a plausible explanation, for instance because a consumer electronics company is exceptionally innovative and has the strongest brand, then perhaps you can rest assured. But if, for instance, a company is selling a mere commodity such as carrots and has no extraordinary competitive advantage to account for a much higher profit margin than others, some kind of accounting fraud may have taken place.

The Organisation Focuses On, And Pays You, Mainly For Recruiting More People

Multi-level marketing (MLM) can be a legitimate and viable business model for the promotion and distribution of a product. For one, it does away with traditional overheads such as rentals in a mall. For another, it taps on the power of social networks, the trust that people have in a recommendation from a friend or relative. If an MLM organisation offers you the chance to make what seems like a realistic profit from selling quality goods to your social network, it can be a good way to make a living or at least supplement your income. In other words, it makes commercial sense to be able to make money that way.

If, however, the organisation has its focus on getting you to 'recruit' more 'members', and pays you mainly for that, your suspicions should certainly be raised. Why are they focusing more on recruitment than the actual sale of the product? Could it mean that their product is really not in demand or is not of high quality? Could it be that they are using the money collected from new members to pay their old members, creating the illusion of profits? You should be even more disturbed if the organisation puts pressure on you to rope in your friends and family members. That would have the hallmarks of a Ponzi scheme where one sucker pulls in five suckers, who then pull in twenty-five, and so on.

Yet another red flag is unrealistically high profit margins from the sale of their products. They may be using revenue from new members to pay you, creating the seductive mirage that their product can generate astonishing profits and motivating you to rave about it to your friends.

A particular tragedy of any scam that drives people to pull in friends and family is that not only will victims lose their hard-earned savings – their most precious relationships will also be left fractured. If you fall victim, your life could lie in ruins – in every conceivable sense.

The Investment Methodology Does Not Make Sense

If you are putting money in a purported investment fund, ask the management company what their investment methodology is (or read it on their website). If it does not make sense to you, or you are unable to at least have a basic understanding of it, it is better to stay away.

Charles Ponzi, the swindler whom 'Ponzi Scheme' was named after, touted an international arbitrage involving buying and selling of coupons redeemable for postage stamps. Apart from its complexity, there weren't enough coupons in existence to use.[5]

The Assets Being Promoted Are In Another Country

An investment instrument may hold assets in a country other than where you live. For instance, you may live in Singapore but the investment instrument's assets may be in Australia or South Africa.

Here we have to distinguish between investments that are listed on the stock exchange and those that are not.

For the latter, I am generally very wary – all the more so if the assets they supposedly hold are overseas. For instance they might be asking you to invest in British land (as in the Profitable

Plots example), a diamond mine in Australia or a sports stadium in Japan. If the asset is so good and attractively priced, the locals would have snapped it up. Why the need to come to your country to market it?

In the case of investments listed on a reputable stock exchange, they are regulated and thus the investor has a significantly higher degree of protection. However, we need to draw a further distinction between companies that are headquartered and listed in your country, and those that come from elsewhere to list in your country. For instance, a company could be headquartered in France and listed in Singapore. An investor would do well to ask more questions about such a firm. Why did it not list in its home market? If there is a convincing reason, for instance, investors in Singapore may be more familiar with its particular industry than investors in its home market and accord it a higher valuation, then perhaps you can trust it. But all too often, crooked individuals list in another country as the people there are less familiar with the assets and it is easier to hoodwink them or, at the very least, sell them an overpriced asset. Furthermore, the authorities in your country may have little ability to enforce their laws and regulations on a company registered elsewhere – and its foreign directors.

If a company is headquartered and listed in your country, holds assets overseas, and is an established company with reputable leaders, then you can invest in it with a higher level of assurance that they will act with a reasonable level of honesty.

The Auditor Is Not Established, Or The Company Won't Tell You Who They Are

Despite supposedly managing US$65 b, Madoff was audited for years not by a major firm but by the three-person accountancy of Friehling & Horowitz in New City, New York[5]. Partner David G. Friehling pleaded guilty to fraud and tax charges, but was sentenced to only one year of home detention and another year of supervised release because he had cooperated extensively with prosecutors and provided testimony that helped to secure convictions for five of Madoff's employees.

If a company or investment scheme won't tell you who their auditors are, it is a red flag.

The Company Does A Lot of Confusing Things

Some rascals try to cheat or at least short-change investors by way of a series of complex and perplexing manoeuvres.

There are listed companies, for example, that engage in one mind-boggling issue after another of rights[6], warrants[7] and/or convertible bonds[8]. Hidden motives may be involved, such as distracting shareholders from unsavoury dealings taking place within the company's business or allowing a connected party to plunder the company's value by granting them convertible bonds on terms that are extremely unfavourable to the existing shareholders.

We must ask hard questions and raise our defences when such manoeuvres take place. Never take the position that "I cannot understand it because I'm stupid – I will just trust the bosses because they're smarter than me" or "they gave me a nice-sounding explanation".

The Company Is Tight-Lipped When Things Go Wrong, But Shouts Out Good News From The Rooftops

I have encountered companies that are very slow and reluctant to disclose that things have gone wrong, and the disclosures are very sketchy. But when they have good results, they take out an ad in the newspapers to blow their horn to the world.

This reveals a serious flaw in character – and some of these companies have later been exposed for misleading shareholders.

For more on how to assess the trustworthiness of a listed company, please read the section "Can you trust these guys?" in Chapter 5.

FURTHER THOUGHTS ON LISTED COMPANIES

As mentioned in Chapter 5, we need to always be mindful when we invest in a company, including listed companies, as a minority or small shareholder because we do not have much say in how the enterprise is run – and are therefore vulnerable to oppression or various forms of misconduct by majority shareholders or the directors and executives whom they choose.

Some Listed Companies: More Monkey Business Than The Zoo

This is not to frighten you away from the stock market, but to give you a real sense of how 'ingenious' some business people and finance professionals can be in using the stock market as an instrument to fleece ordinary people. My next intermediate goal is to drive home the importance of assessing the integrity of the directors and executives behind a listed enterprise; my ultimate goal, of course, is to help you become a better investor and achieve financial freedom.

Here are a few accounts of such schemes – some anecdotal, but all quite believable in the real world of business and finance. A company headquartered in a different country from where it was listed reported that its accounts had disappeared because the truck that was transporting them had been stolen. Another company invited analysts and prospective investors to visit its purported farm, and when one of the visitors chatted with a worker on that farm, the worker said he had never heard of the company – even though the signboard at the entrance bore its name.

A now (in)famous article circulating on the Internet is titled 'Confessions of an S-chip CEO'. S-chips are mainland Chinese firms listed on the Singapore Exchange. They flocked to Singapore to list in the noughties; many were accepted by the Exchange; and sadly, dozens of them were caught for accounting irregularities, governance lapses and various kinds of fraud. Many were suspended and then delisted with no compensation to shareholders, leaving thousands of Singaporeans poorer. While there is no way to verify whether the article is fictitious, it certainly offers a plausible depiction of the motivations and methods behind these predatory deceptions.

In the article, the protagonist and narrator is a relatively young Chinese executive who has worked at a textile corporation for some years and is impatient to take over from his older colleagues. He is introduced to a 'dealmaker' who claims he can get the company listed in Singapore. The protagonist and his colleagues and fellow shareholders are very keen to unlock the value of their stakes in the firm and become 'paper millionaires' in a booming China.

Even though the company is growing at a steady rate, it is not exciting enough to make the initial public offering (IPO) a sure-win. So the dealmaker, probably drawing on his extensive connections, gets investment funds to pump in fresh capital to help the company produce a new type of artificial fibre. Customers find it attractive, but are not willing to commit in case their customers do not like products made with this new yarn. The dealmaker then suggests pushing the products to customers by offering them very attractive, longer payment terms, and the company plays along – artificially boosting sales numbers. Later on, the business goes as far as to practically give their fibres to customers, telling them they do not need to pay until their products are sold. The company then books these sales as receivables.

These tricks make the company's sales numbers look very impressive. The dealmaker convinces the company owners to let the protagonist be promoted to CEO as a younger and more dynamic face is needed to front the company. They manage to assuage the concerns of the exchange officials and the company is listed.

After that, greed swells to unmanageable proportions in the 'CEO' as he makes a killing investing in stocks, often based on his connection with the dealmaker who helps him get into 'exciting' new companies and IPOs on the ground floor. He also ploughs money into properties. Banks are very eager to lend to the 'CEO' to finance his heavy investments. Money keeps making more money, and the 'CEO' and his friends feel like "Masters of the Universe".

Abruptly, in 2008, the Global Financial Crisis strikes, causing him serious problems as his investments plummet. He has trouble paying off his loans and cannot resist the temptation to dip his hands into his company's honey jug ... and the rest is history. When the company gets into trouble with the auditors, he flees back to China where he is immune to any prosecution for his misdeeds in Singapore, as the two countries do not have an established bilateral extradition treaty.

One particularly disturbing quote from the article is what the 'dealmaker' supposedly told our protagonist: "Water enough money into any company, (and) even a fake one could become real some day."

Just as disturbing was a conversation with a streetwise friend who shared in a most sober way with me that many corporate leaders actually make more money manipulating their stock (probably using friends as proxies, so it is difficult to trace these activities to the boss) than they do from the business itself. There are many ways to fool the market into buying or selling a stock – for instance, making a misleading announcement that the company is in talks with parties interested to take it over, or doing some creative accounting to make a quarterly result look worse than it actually is.

But let us not be frightened off investing in stocks. As with the people we deal with in everyday life, there are good eggs and bad eggs in the stock market. We just have to develop a strong vigilance and a healthy level of scepticism. If we exercise these, together with Common Sense, and carry out sensible tests such as the ones described in Chapter 5 (see the section titled 'Can you trust these guys?'), we have a good chance of avoiding the snares laid by unscrupulous businessmen and financiers – and putting our money to work in honest, thriving enterprises.

Do your due diligence before parting with your precious money in this dangerous world. You owe it to yourself and your family. Know your rights as a shareholder and what recourse is available to you if there is impropriety.

SHAREHOLDERS' RIGHTS AND REMEDIES IN SINGAPORE

Shareholders' Rights

Right to information

A company is required to keep information about its shareholders, directors and financials at its registered office. All shareholders have the right to have access to these documents – including to inspect the registry for certain personal information and the roles of the directors, secretaries, managers, and auditors. A shareholder can also ask for the directors' shareholdings in the company and any other corporations (if there are).[9] She is also entitled to request and be furnished within fourteen days with a copy of the minutes of general meetings.

Right to attend general meetings

All shareholders have the right to attend any general meeting of the corporation. They are also free to speak at the event. In fact, a minority shareholder can even call for an extraordinary general meeting (EGM) to, for instance, remove a director from the Board.

According to Section 177(1) of the Companies Act, a group of two or more shareholders holding a combined stake of not less than 10 percent of the total number of issued shares of the company (excluding treasury shares) can call for an EGM without the prior approval of the Board. Moreover, under Section 183 of the same Act, members representing 5 percent or more of the total voting rights, or not fewer than 100 members holding shares in the company on which there has been paid up an average sum, per member, of not less than $500, may requisition the company to give to members notice of any resolution that may properly be moved and is intended to be moved at any general meeting.

Right to fair treatment

Lastly, a company should treat all its shareholders fairly. If a minority shareholder feels that he/she has been unfairly treated by the directors or the company, he/she has the right to seek redress from a court of law. But, the shareholder has to understand that the cost of any legal battles need not be covered by the company.

Examples of unfair treatment or minority oppression include:

(a) an unreasonable dilution of minority shares

(b) an unreasonable exclusion from management

(c) an unreasonable refusal to pay dividends

(d) a change in the nature of the business without receiving shareholders' consent

An alternative to filing a case in court is to approach a shareholders' association or activist group to take up your grievances with the company or mediate in your dispute.

If, however, you do go to court, the following remedies are provided for under the Companies Act.

Remedies Under Singapore Law

Injunctive and directive relief

Where it deems fit, the court has the power to direct or prohibit any act, or cancel or vary any transaction or resolution[10].

For example, the court may order the company:

(a) to hold or to refrain from holding a general meeting

(b) to pass or to refrain from passing resolutions

(c) to undo any improper transactions

Regulation of corporate affairs

Specific orders which add to, modify or vary the articles of association of a company may be given by the court where such orders would remedy past irregularities and allow the company to operate on a regular basis in the future.

Examples of specific orders include:

(a) appointing the board of directors chosen by the court

(b) ruling that the company's bank accounts must be operated with the signatures of two directors

Damages

The court may order the wrongdoer to compensate the minority shareholder for the loss sustained, in the form of damages, where it is clear from the evidence that such loss arose from the wrongdoer's acts.

If the cause and the quantum of the loss cannot be definitively ascertained, the court is unlikely to order for damages.

Buy-out

Where the company is deemed to be still viable, a possible remedy is an order for the purchase of the shares of the minority shareholder by the company.

On the basis that the company is a going concern, the shares of the minority shareholder will be valued on the date on which they were ordered to be purchased. The valuation must be fair and just on the facts of the case. What is fair and just is for the court to decide.

Winding up

The court can also call for the winding up of the company as an order of last resort for an oppression application. Such a drastic measure is usually resorted to in a situation where the deadlock in the management has reached such a level that other types of remedies would have little practical effect.

Order to commence proceedings in the name of the company

The court may order for a derivative action under Section 216A of the Companies Act to be pursued where the alleged oppression is due to acts resulting in loss to the company. Any relief granted by the court will therefore be for the benefit of the company and not the individual shareholder.

The Companies Act, however, applies only to Singapore-registered companies. Before investing in a company, do take a look at the country of incorporation. Once it is non-Singapore – for instance, a Chinese, German or Cayman Islands entity – your level of protection goes down several notches and you have little say or recourse if some kind of impropriety were to take place. This is not to say that it is definitely a bad apple or poor investment, just that it is a risk factor to be aware of.

As I am based in Singapore, I have discussed the remedies available under Singapore law but if you live or invest in another country, I certainly encourage you to do some research online about the legal options in the relevant jurisdiction(s). It is an important part of due diligence. Always do your homework.

And don't believe some investment sales pitch just because it comes from a famous footballer!

1   According to Deputy Public Prosecutor Luke Tan's statements to the court, as mentioned in "I lost more than $200K in UK land investment, now I work as a security guard" by Leong Chan Teik, Nextinsight (website), 20 Feb 2016.

2   "Profitable Plots investor sues to get her $31,500 back", *TODAY* newspaper, 1 June 2010.

3   According to Wikipedia, a Ponzi scheme is a fraudulent investment operation where the operator provides fabricated reports and generates returns for older investors through revenue paid by new investors, rather than from legitimate business activities or profit of financial trading. Operators of Ponzi schemes can be either individuals or corporations, and grab the attention of new investors by offering short-term returns that are either abnormally high or unusually consistent.

4   Chew, Robert (4 Feb, 2009). "A Madoff Whistle-Blower Tells His Story". *TIME*. http://content.time.com/time/business/article/0,8599,1877181,00.html.

5   "In Pictures: 10 Warning Signs Of A Ponzi Scam". Forbes, June 12, 2010. https://www.forbes.com/2010/06/09/madoff-starr-scam-investment-fraud-personal-finance-10-warning-signs-ponzi_slide/

6   A rights issue is an issue of new shares offered at a special price by a company to its existing shareholders in proportion to their holding of old shares. (Source: Oxford Dictionary)

7   A warrant is similar to an option, giving the holder the right but not the obligation to buy an underlying security at a certain price, quantity and future time. It's unlike an option in that a warrant is issued by a company, whereas an option is an instrument offered by a central exchange. The

security represented in the warrant (usually share equity) is delivered by the issuing company instead of a counter-party holding the shares. (Source: Investopedia)

8   A convertible bond is a type of debt security that can be converted into a predetermined amount of the underlying company's equity at certain times during the bond's life, usually at the discretion of the bondholder. (Source: Investopedia)

9   "Do you know your rights as a minority shareholder?", Stanley Lim Peir Sheng, Motley Fool Singapore (website), 27 May 2016. Accessed 13 Jun 2018. https://www.fool.sg/2016/05/27/do-you-know-your-rights-as-a-minority-shareholder/

10 "Oppression of Minority Shareholders", Singapore Legal Advice (website), last updated 27 Nov 2015. Accessed 13 Jun 2018. https://singaporelegaladvice.com/law-articles/oppression-of-minority-shareholders.

FINANCIAL INDEPENDENCE IS KEY TO ATTAINING LASTING HAPPINESS FOR YOU AND YOUR FAMILY

I am writing this on my mobile device as I walk along the park connector that follows the Geylang River in Singapore. The old, dirty river has been transformed into a beautiful, active waterway that links the fast-rising Paya Lebar Regional Centre to the new Sports Hub built on part of the old Kallang Airport.

Here, the Geylang River enters the Kallang Basin and melds with the Kallang River which has wound its way from the Lower Peirce Reservoir. Kallang Basin itself was a filthy area in the 1960s, with hardly any fish in waters polluted by rubbish thrown by various users, including the small boat builders in Tanjong Rhu that fronted the Basin.

Now, there is a sea change. The relatively clean water harbours plenty of fish to the delight of the many anglers as well as otters that have made a reappearance after decades missing-in-action. My thoughts flow as I walk the landscaped Tanjong Rhu area transformed into a popular residential enclave.

Two old rivers originating from different sources and they eventually meet to produce a beautiful basin that is now part of the Marina Reservoir in the heart of the city. One can't differentiate the waters in the basin.

Investing and entrepreneurship are also two different sources of water – or wealth if you like – that eventually produce an indistinguishable end product: financial independence.

Financial independence is a higher state than merely saving enough for retirement. It requires harder work and much discipline so that eventually the individual or family is able to live entirely on passive dividend or interest income, while the principal amount remains intact and growing on capital gains.

Which road you take, investment or entrepreneurship, turns on your situation in early adulthood. It depends on your family background, financial situation, education level and, most importantly, your own attitude to work and life.

Quite often, but not always, entrepreneurship is born out of necessity. My own observation is that young people who are less strong in academic studies or who do not have a chance to go for higher education, will opt to do business of some sort. They may enter the workforce at an early age and learn some skill or business while earning a modest salary.

After a few years on a steep learning curve, they move out on their own to start a small business in their area of knowledge. Often, while at work, they discover their strengths in terms of skills and attributes. These are put to good use in building the business and earning a living. But it is very tough going, at least in the initial stages.

Being an entrepreneur means you have no certainty of income and no guarantee of tenure as in a secure job in a large company or in the public sector. Even small and medium companies offer more job security and predictability of income than a small business.

It is also lonely being a small entrepreneur as you cannot share your problems with most people. Spouses need to be supportive and understanding, and entrepreneurs have to be sure their families will stand by them through thick and thin. It can mean long working days with no meaningful breaks and no financial cushion during difficult times.

Most young Singaporeans opt for the career route upon completing their studies. Their parents slog to make sure they get a good education and spend vast sums on private tuition to ensure they do well. Getting a university degree is a popular, some would say necessary, aspiration for young citizens.

Once the degree is in the bag, the next goal is to build a career in an established private entity or the government sector. They start work in their mid- or late-twenties and those who work hard and apply themselves usually enjoy career advancement and rising salaries over the years.

By the time they hit forty years of age, many such employees would be comfortably ensconced in their jobs and careers and supporting nuclear families while paying off their property mortgages. They may harbour visions of being their own bosses but it becomes difficult to move out due to the uncertainty of entrepreneurship.

So most young people who opt for careers upon graduating hold on to their jobs. They may switch companies and take on adjacent responsibilities but their dreams of embarking on an entrepreneurial road dim with age. As the family grows, so do the expenses and it becomes too risky to leave a lucrative career for the unpredictability of business.

The goal of the career man or lady is to build savings for retirement. Most people do not want to work their entire lives and they also know that the risk of being laid off increases as one moves up the career ladder. This is because employers often do not hesitate to hire a younger person or persons who can do the same job or jobs for much less than the old timers.

If you have taken the career route, it is fine. You just need to ensure you exercise financial discipline when the going is good and build up your savings, insurance and investments. While holding your job, do spend time to learn about these three prongs of financial planning and how to attain good results in the long term.

Do not regret losing the opportunity to be an entrepreneur and/or your own boss. Even as an avid value investor who takes a keen interest in the stocks that you hold, you are actually a partner to the business. Understand the intricacies of the business and where possible, offer ideas to the entrepreneur running the company.

I started as a young journalist in the *Business Times* in 1977. Being a science graduate, I knew little about business. But I learnt along the way, not only about what makes businesses tick, but also their accounts and balance sheets. I progressed rapidly as a journalist and as my seniority advanced to the position of Chief Editor, so did my income.

It became difficult for me to make a great leap into the unknown, in starting a business. I knew there was a good chance my business would prosper eventually, but the thought of a massive loss of income for some years was worrying. So I stayed in secure jobs in Singapore Press Holdings and later in DBS and MediaCorp.

I finished as editor-in-chief and CEO of the *TODAY* newspaper in 2006. Over thirty years, I saved and invested enough to attain financial independence in 2005 when I reached fifty-five years of age.

Chapters 1, 4 and 5 of this book tell you how you can attain financial independence or get substantially there with hard work and financial discipline from a young age.

But just as the Geylang River leads to the beautiful and resource-rich Kallang Basin, so does the Kallang River which takes a different route.

As an entrepreneur, you apply your mind to making your business grow. That's your life, your career. Day-in and day-out, you will encounter problems. It could be an increase in government taxes or your landlord wanting to squeeze you harder on the rental payable. You may find it difficult to hire good staff or, worse, experienced staff start leaving you for greener pastures. New competition may make your business less viable or technology may emerge to disrupt your way of making money.

I did a study of 35 companies in 2012 with the objective of understanding their success factors over a span of thirty years. These were established companies listed on the Singapore Exchange. They included Kingsmen Creatives, BreadTalk and Rotary Engineering. I interviewed the CEOs and CFOs and visited their operations.

What made them succeed where many others fell by the wayside? What did these entrepreneurs have that others did not? Was it their superior products or the pricing policy or the brand names? Were they better at managing their people or was it their management of finances and cashflow that ensured their survival and growth?

I found that all these factors were important in the success of a business over the long term. But the common thread that ran through all 35 companies was that they were run by people who were good problem-solvers. These entrepreneurs basically took any problem that came along and applied their minds to resolve it. Hundreds, if not thousands, of difficulties were encountered on the path to eventual success as a sizeable and profitable company. They had to be systematically overcome by the entrepreneur and his management team. Every worker also played a part in helping the company along.

If you're a successful entrepreneur owning a major part of a sizeable company, then you are well on the way, if not on top already, of being financially independent. Many entrepreneurs stumble at some point and their businesses run into the ground. Some pick themselves up and start all over again, learning from past mistakes. Others stay poor for the rest of their lives.

But again, they are not that different from the employees or career persons who succeeded or failed in their endeavours to attain eventual financial independence. There are those career persons who fail to keep up with trends in their professions and end up being laid off from their jobs. That can be traumatic and upset any financial plans set in place. Financial independence can become an elusive goal.

So, ultimately, there is no short cut to success. This may sound like a motherhood statement but I believe in it. There is no running away from treating life as a marathon and aiming to succeed in the long run rather than in short sprints along the way. Whichever route you take, the entrepreneur or the career person, you have to stay on top of your chosen profession or business.

Take problems as they come and learn to resolve them to the best of your ability. Even if the solutions are not perfect. Move ahead to seize other opportunities. As your income improves, do not switch to ostentatious lifestyles. Maintain financial discipline and save for the future. Keep reserves for the difficult times that must come in everyone's lives.

It will not be easy to complete the marathon of life in good shape. You have to work and train for it and keep faith that whatever path or route you take, it will lead you to the desired goal. The discipline and restraint exercised will be well worth the final result.

They say happiness is all in the mind. It is a state of mind, a conscious choice. You can decide if you're happy or otherwise. That is true to some extent. But I think financial freedom helps you to achieve the right state of mind. It takes you beyond the daily grind of earning a living and ensuring the well-being of your loved ones. You feel more confident about yourself and that shows in the way you interact with your friends and acquaintances. You have a firmer handshake, knowing you depend on no one.

Successful entrepreneurs show this quality or attribute. Self-confidence. As an employee who evolves into a successful investor, you will enjoy that too. It is an aura that surrounds people who have freed themselves from modern day slavery. I hope this book will play a part in getting you there. Lasting happiness for you and your family.

ABOUT THE AUTHOR

Mano Sabnani is currently the Chairman and CEO of Rafflesia Holdings, a company he founded in 2008 to pursue opportunities in the investment, corporate advisory and media sectors.

He was invited to serve as an adjunct professor at SIM University from January 2011 to April 2016, and also as advisor to the Centre for Applied Research (CFAR) where he completed a project involving the preparation of 35 case studies of Singapore companies listed on the SGX.

Earlier in his career, Mano worked in senior positions in Singapore's *Business Times* (writing and editing on a variety of investment and business issues as well as politics and foreign affairs) and the Development Bank of Singapore (developing investment products for the bank's many medium-to-high net-worth clients; leading a team of analysts to produce reports on the best stocks, bonds and warrants in the Singapore stock market; and preparing numerous companies for a public listing and successful launch on the SGX as an MD at the bank's Equity Capital Markets). At Corporate Brokers International where he was executive director, he focused on nurturing and investing in small, promising companies with scaleable businesses, and as MediaCorp's CEO and Editor-in-Chief, he developed the daily newspaper *TODAY* into the second most read in Singapore and made it very profitable by the time he left in November 2006.

A well-known activist investor, financial writer and advisor, Mano is active in the press and social media as a writer and commentator. He is a successful value investor himself and strongly believes in every individual working towards financial freedom, and has led seminars and spoken extensively about investment and financial planning.

Mano graduated from the University of Singapore (now the National University of Singapore) with a Bachelor of Science degree majoring in Physics. He attended the Advanced Management Programme at INSEAD Business School (France) in 1990 and the Press Fellowship programme at Wolfson College, Cambridge (UK), in 1986.

He has authored several books, including his autobiography *Marbles, Mayhem and my Typewriter.*